CROSSING THE LINE

CROSSING
the LINE

A Bluejacket's World War II Odyssey

ALVIN KERNAN

NAVAL INSTITUTE PRESS
Annapolis, Maryland

BLUEJACKET BOOKS

©1994, 1997
by the United States Naval Institute
Annapolis, Maryland

First Bluejacket Books printing, 1997
ISBN 1-55750-461-X

Unless noted otherwise, all photos courtesy of the author.
The Library of Congress has cataloged the hardcover edition as follows:
Kernan, Alvin B.

    Crossing the line: a bluejacket's World War II odyssey / by Alvin Kernan.

      p.   cm.

    Includes index.

    ISBN 1-55750-455-5

    1. Kernan, Alvin B. 2. World War, 1939–1945—Naval operations, American.
3. World War, 1939–1945—Personal narratives, American. 4. Seamen—United
States—Biography. 5. United States. Navy—Biography. I. Title.
D773.K46   1994
940.54'5973—dc20   94-16547

Printed in the United States of America on acid-free paper ∞

04 03 02 01 00 99   8 7 6 5 4 3 2

For my children

If you would travel farther than all travelers . . . start now on that
farthest western way, which does not pause at the Mississippi or the Pacific,
nor conduct toward a worn-out China or Japan, but leads on direct, a
tangent to this sphere, summer and winter, day and night, sun down, moon
down, and at last earth down too.

—Henry David Thoreau, *Walden*

CONTENTS

FOREWORD

My qualifications for writing an introduction to Alvin Kernan's remarkably vivid, frank, and moving description of his experiences in the navy during World War II are as follows. After serving in several ships from a destroyer to a battleship, I too ended up, like Kernan, in an escort carrier in the western Pacific off Japan. We were both part of the Seventh Fleet, which was the greatest battle fleet ever assembled, under the command of Admiral Nimitz, and the most amazingly efficient organization I have ever seen in my life. My aircraft carrier, HMS *Chaser*, had been sent to serve in the Pacific, partly to help the Americans but mostly to make sure that, in a fit of anticolonial enthusiasm, they did not give Hong Kong back to the Chinese at the end of the war. In this we were successful, being the first ship to enter the harbor after the Japanese surrender.

Kernan and I joined our respective navies from noticeably different backgrounds. He was abruptly wrenched out of civilian life on a remote, isolated ranch in Wyoming and thrown into the traumatic experience of boot camp. I was similarly wrenched out of civilian life, but in my case this meant cozy rooms, good food, and a servant to wait on me, all of which were provided to prewar students at Oxford University. After boot camp at Shotley and nine months on the lower deck of HMS *Fiji*, I was sent back home for officer training and thereafter served in the comfortable, if alcoholic, atmosphere of a British naval officers' wardroom.

Kernan saw much action, exhibited great bravery, and was many times very nearly killed; once he even had to abandon his sinking ship. Although I was involved in several dangerous operations, including two convoys to Malta and two to Murmansk, my life was in imminent danger only once. Kernan served as a gunner on a plane, frequently in fierce combat, while I sat in a windowless office as senior aircraft controller, directing planes like his to their missions. But as I read his story, again and again I find myself thinking: yes, this is *exactly* how it was.

The author encapsulates the culture and ideology of the U.S. Navy of that time in a series of shrewd observations. For example, "Cleanliness was not next to godliness in the United States Navy; it was godliness." Boot camp, with its endless drill on the "grinder," was designed to force you "to put your individuality in storage. . . . reasonable excuses were not part of this life." For me, on the other hand, the benefits of low cunning were also part of boot camp. I soon made an arrangement with the chief petty officer by which I would take charge of our squad after 1600, leaving him free to go home. In exchange, he left me alone all day—time which I spent reading Proust in the laundry (the only place where I could be both warm and safe from discovery).

The culture of the U.S. Navy as described by Kernan is identical with that to be found in the British navy of the same period. More remarkable is the similar inefficiency of our navies' planes and, especially, the torpedoes with which both fleets were provided in the early stages of the war. (When I complained to a senior officer, he retorted that British torpedoes were excellent in peacetime—that is, on maneuvers—since they could be relied upon to come to the surface after firing and so to be used again!) Only the Japanese and the Germans seem to have been able to manufacture effective torpedoes. In the end, victory came from the sheer volume of military hardware, plus advanced radar, success in decoding, and, as at the Battle of Midway, to which Kernan devotes a riveting chapter, a lot of luck.

Kernan notes the brutality of life as a seaman during wartime, a life he describes as "healthy but in many respects like a chain gang." He reminds us that in times of crisis all hands were on four-hour shifts (four on, four off) throughout the day and night, so that one was perpetually tired. He also remembers the torments of heat rash in the tropics. Nor does he ever forget that "death lived on an aircraft carrier operating in wartime conditions." One day a plane would crash on takeoff; the next day a plane would crash on landing. And it was all too easy for one of the flight deck crew to take a false step and get chewed up by a propeller.

Sometimes "planes went out on patrol and were never heard of again." This was a particular agony to me, as I called the plane for hours on the radio and listened as the signals became fainter and fainter, ending in a total silence.

Kernan rightly lays great stress on the sheer boredom of life during the long stretches between the brief moments of sheer terror. He describes how the Americans spent their time playing cards for money, often all day long.

It was mostly poker, and the gambling was for high stakes. The British did the same, but the stakes were very much lower. We could never have pulled off Kernan's last financial coup. We tended to play liar's dice, the loser buying drinks all round, and for a while we played endless games of Monopoly. The conversation, such as it was, was mostly about sex and girls, if only because they were in such short supply.

The author deals discreetly but frankly with the sexual problems and temptations for young sailors on periods of leave. Prostitutes were readily available in every naval base, but they were not always free from venereal disease. I do not know what happened in the Pacific theater, since our rear base was Sydney, Australia, but in the Mediterranean theater—in Algiers, Naples, Rome, etc.—the U.S. Army tried to deal with this problem by organizing medically supervised brothels, some for officers and others for enlisted men, as so vividly described in Joseph Heller's *Catch 22*. A young man has to lose his virginity some time, and Kernan observes that "sex and war really initiate us into society," while the former provides some intense pleasure "in a world that offers a lot of dullness and pain."

But Kernan does not fail to mention the good times and the nobler aspects of a sailor's life in wartime. For example, "the instant love affair" with whatever ship one happened to be assigned to. He observes, correctly, that "to a young man war is exciting." At that age—eighteen, nineteen, twenty—we all thought that we were immortal. It was only the older men, worried about a wife and children, who were constantly afraid of death. There was no great hostility toward the Japanese, who, rightly, "were regarded as a worthy foe." Taken all in all, "we saw the war as a natural and rare chance to live life at least close to something great." The Seventh Fleet off Japan was one of the most amazing sights we would ever behold—a gigantic armada spread out over miles and miles of ocean, the vast assembly all dedicated to the destruction of Tokyo and Japan. At night, the phosphorescence of the water all around us was all that was visible of this stupendous array of warships.

This "handbook to life" is a brilliantly evocative, scrupulously honest, and extremely well-written description of naval life on the lower deck in World War II, comparable only, so far as I know, to the equally distinguished memoir of another aviator turned scholar, Samuel Hynes. If anyone wants to know what it was really like to serve in the U.S. Navy in World War II, these are the books to read.

Lawrence Stone
Princeton, New Jersey

PREFACE *to the Bluejacket Books Edition*

It was once the custom, perhaps still is, when a young man enlisted in the United States Navy to issue him a small soft-covered blue book titled *The Bluejackets' Manual*. This book did not come for free. Several dollars were deducted on the first payday for it. It was impossible to manage without this little handbook whose chapters A to N covered such seaman's skills as tying knots (square or Turk's head), reading signal flags (Able, Baker, Charley), wearing your hat and when not, saluting correctly, and shipping oars smartly.

Since the chapters stopped at N, recruits used to speculate about what the chapters that came after N in *The Bluejackets' Manual* covered. Perhaps there were no chapters beyond N; perhaps A to N covered everything known or necessary to be known about naval life. This view was not favored, however, and mysteries grew up around chapters O to Z. These chapters, it was said by some, were for officers only, and covered the duties and pleasures of those strange and distant creatures. Others said that these chapters dealt with special skills such as boilermaking, sheet metal work, torpedo preparation, and quartermasters' responsibilities. With the growing understanding that it was better in the navy never to ask questions, no one I knew ever inquired officially about O to Z, and the content of these remarkable chapters remained a mystery.

It may be, of course, that chapters O through Z exist in numerous copies read every day by someone. But in time I came to feel privately that the navy in its wisdom had reserved O to Z for the sailor's personal experiences: all those things that a young man had to learn about life, as we used to say, "the hard way." They couldn't be written down because they were not the same for any two people, and because no one ever believed what someone else told him about these matters. No doubt that is still true. What could have changed it?

Still, I like to think of my memories of life on the aircraft carriers in what the Japanese call the Great Pacific War as a "Bluejackets' Manual, Chapters O to Z," which others may find amusing to compare with their own handbooks of life.

The reader may wonder from time to time how it was possible for me, after fifty years, to remember so precisely some details, such as the pay grades for apprentice seaman, seaman second class, and seaman first class. I can only say that these matters were so deeply and powerfully imprinted on my mind that they remain fresh and vivid to this day. Frequently I discovered that things I did not remember consciously would come flooding back in detailed pictures as I began to sketch in a scene on the word processor, flowing, as it were, out of my fingertips.

Others have their memories too, and the publication of *Crossing the Line* brought a flood of letters from men—not many women—who remembered the events I described, though often in a different way. An intelligence officer wrote that my story about the plans for Midway circulating by scuttlebutt on the *Enterprise* a month before the battle simply could not have been true since it was the war's best-kept secret. I could merely reply that on this matter my memory was firm and clear. Another writer told me about finding Al Capone's armored Cadillac limousine in Shanghai after the war ended. Vice Adm. William D. Houser, USN (Ret.), wrote that he had been in the antiaircraft batteries on the USS *Nashville* when it fired on the Japanese picketboats encountered as the *Hornet* was about to launch the Doolittle raiders on Tokyo. I had referred to the failure of nearly a thousand six-inch shells to sink the pickets as "disgraceful." Admiral Houser took exception to this term, explaining that "*Nashville* opened fire at long range on the wildly tossing craft and scored a number of hits. The gunfire straddled the small wooden ships, but the shells were all armor-piercing and thus hits passed through without exploding." Admiral Houser also sent a copy of his letter and my book to Rear Adm. Harry Mason, USN (Ret.), who just happened to have been the fire control officer on the *Nashville* that day. He thought my story sounded like one told by Sinbad the sailor in the *Arabian Nights' Entertainments*.

The most evocative letters came from shipmates of half a century ago who had stored away in their heads some of the same scenes I had in mine. Imagine opening a letter to read, "I recall you and I standing up on the hangar deck of CV-8 [the *Hornet*] waiting to climb down the cargo net to the deck of the DD-410, *Hughes*. While in line, you asked me if there was anything I wanted from my locker. I said, 'Kernan, I wouldn't go back below for anything.' You insisted on going—you came back with a pillow cover with my gear." This was my old shipmate Dan Vanderhoof, not seen or heard from for fifty years.

I had last seen Hazen Rand—the radar officer in my plane the night Butch O'Hare was killed—as he was carried off to sick bay with a Japanese bullet in his foot. Now his letter told me that the wound had taken years to heal, that he had caught some kind of crud in the hospital that was cured only when he, painted blue all over with fungicide, was immersed to the waist in a barrel of gasoline. It had, I learned, taken fifty years for his Navy Cross to catch up with him, and then the Navy Department sent him two. But he still remembered vividly that wild night when the *Enterprise*'s Black Panthers drove the Japanese air fleet away from our ships: "Butch got lost and sought enlightenment by turning on recognition lights in front of a Japanese bomber. The Jap shot up Butch's can and Al Kernan shot the Jap."

Some voices even came back from the dead. I had written about three bodies stretched out on the deck of the USS *Suwanee* after one of its own hundred-pound bombs exploded on landing. Then came a letter from Dick Morrow, the gunner, who had spent a long and happy life directing a fashionable dance orchestra in the suburbs of Detroit. "I had no idea what had happened until the flames began to burn me. . . . I remember releasing the turret window latch and falling out. . . . I also remember hearing 'Taps' over the ship's loudspeaker at the moment Obie [the pilot, Lt. (junior grade) O. B. Slingerland] was being buried at sea. . . . Then, while on a landing barge, I heard a medical corpsman exclaim that Jim Joyce's [the radioman's] tongue was swollen and he had passed away."

Crossing the Line brought into view a whole star field of images hitherto hidden in the minds of former sailors. Often children whose fathers had mentioned only brief events in the war wrote to find out what it had actually been like the day the *Hornet* sank, or when Lieutenant Collura went down on the way back from Ishigaki. Occasionally people who had never heard how their relative died wrote to ask me for information. "I am the widow of John Wiley Brock, who was . . . in VT-6 on the old *Enterprise*, and was killed in 1942 at Midway. . . . What I would like to know is, do you remember him? I have never found anyone who did. I would like this information for our son . . . who never knew his father." Others, "old salts" who had nearly forgotten the paint chipper, the green plush on the seats of the troop trains, or the smell of the recreation center on Mog Mog, wrote that *Crossing the Line* brought it all back to life for at least a moment, and they were moved enough to write and reminisce with me for a few pages. I think a writer can hope for no better use of his book.

Alvin Kernan
Princeton, New Jersey

ONE

Home

In the winter of 1941, I stood in snow that was over my head in the mountains of south-central Wyoming and realized it wasn't going to work. Our ranch was five miles from the nearest neighbor, and during five months of the year we had to snowshoe or ski that five miles, leaving the car and carrying in packs or pulling on sleds whatever supplies were necessary until the next month when we went to town again, about twenty miles away. We cut enough wood in summer to keep the stoves burning and stored enough staples in a cave dug into the mountainside to see us through the winter. There was no electricity or running water. The horses were driven down the valley and boarded for the winter with people who lived out of the shadow of the mountain, where the snows were the heaviest. I boarded in town while I went to school. Usually there were just three of us, my mother, stepfather, and myself, plus a few dogs and cats, the cats all brown and singed on their sides from spending their days trying to keep warm curled around the stovepipes where they came out of the roof.

The ranch had been one of the last homesteads taken out and "proved up," 640 acres in a canyon near the head of South Spring Creek, eighty-five hundred feet high, a few miles below the crest of the Continental Divide, south of the little town of Saratoga in the valley of the North Platte where the young river comes out of the Colorado mountains into southern Wyoming. It was an intensely real place, water, sagebrush, rocks, pine trees, but the ranch was also a dream, my stepfather's dream, after he lost his job in the Depression, that a Wyoming dude ranch would provide a wonderful life for all of us and eventually make us rich. As in every other American family during the Depression, conversations frequently began with "When we get rich . . ." The ranch neither made us rich nor provided the life we dreamed of, and there was never the slightest chance that it would work with no capital to build it, no fish or

Winter 1941, Main Street, Saratoga, Wyoming—twenty miles from our ranch—
where I went to school.

game big enough to attract dudes, and no dudes with enough money or interest to find their way to a small rundown ranch forty miles from a railroad or a
paved highway.

My stepfather couldn't see it, of course; he had no place else to go. But a
wind that would knock you off your feet, snow eight feet deep, and weeks of
below-zero weather were sharpening up my thinking. Perhaps the conclusive
experience came in early November 1940. I had graduated from high school
that year and, not being able to get a job, was staying on the ranch alone
taking care of things, my stepfather away in the east looking for work, my
mother with him. The snows had held off longer than usual, and one day an
old car, a Star coupe, a brand by then no longer known or sold, pulled up
and stopped in front of the fence, waiting. No one got out for a while. It was a
time and place when it was not thought polite to be too forward, and I
waited before going down to lean on the fence, establishing ownership, and
say hello. By then two men and a pregnant woman were out of the car. They
wanted to know the condition of the road above our ranch, a road that ran
for about ten miles through the Medicine Bow National Forest up to a lake,
South Spring Creek Lake, in the core of an old volcano, its peak part of the
Continental Divide, with one side blown out, Mount St. Helens fashion, out
of which ran South Spring Creek, down the canyon in which our ranch was
located, and then on out onto the plain and some twenty miles farther to
the North Platte River.

The road, built by miners years ago and not maintained, at the best of times was definitely unimproved, over big rocks, through swamps, dugways nearly washed away in the side of mountains, across rotting log bridges, and, in places, up 40-degree slopes. I told them that the bridges, though shaky, had all still been there a week ago when I had gone deer hunting up that way, but that they would need something powerful, flexible, and high centered to get up the road. All things their antique car was not. They went off together and talked for a while and then came back and asked if I would take them by wagon to an old mine a mile or so above the lake up on the shoulder of Mount Vulcan, one of the peaks of the divide. They were miners, and they wanted to get a sense of the state of the old mine shaft and take out some of the equipment that had been left there, mainly a couple of rock drills.

The weather was not good, and the snow likely to begin anytime, which I told them, adding the truth that once it began at this time of year, you could get snowed in all winter. They still wanted to go, and I sensed that there might be real money in this job, so I gulped and said I would go for ten dollars. I had never had ten dollars at once, and they too were impressed with the big money we were talking. They were out of work, hoping to find a mine and work it themselves for enough ore to sell to some smelter in Colorado to keep going, always with the hope of a real strike. We were all

Vulcan Mountain and the crest of the Continental Divide. The old workings to which I took the miners are at the foot of the draw leading to the peak.

dreamers then! Since they were nearly broke, they bargained hard, starting at five dollars, moving to seven, and agreeing to ten when I remained adamant, knowing nothing about bargaining, only if I would feed them, let them sleep there that night, and allow the pregnant woman to stay in the cabin while we were gone.

Feeling like a real entrepreneur, the next morning before light I had the old team out—I should have taken them down the valley weeks before—the wagon hitched, with some oats for the horses in a sack, and off we went, with the smell of snow in the air. The road had never been worse, but we jolted along, and I worried away about whether my stepfather would ever find out, and if he did, would he want half of the money for wear and tear on the horses and the wagon, or would he just be plain mad about my doing something with his property without permission.

With enough snow on the ground to make the rocks slick, the going was slower than usual, and dark came in that deepening canyon at that time of year before four in the afternoon. Shortly after a lunchless noon, we got stuck in a narrow place trying to turn between some close rocks. The only wagon box we had was sixteen feet long. A shorter one, on a short reach, would have been much better for this work, and the long wagon was firmly wedged. After some geeing and hawing it was clear that the only way to get out of there was to unhitch the horses, take off the wagon box, disassemble the wagon, and put it together facing the opposite way, downhill and back toward the ranch.

The miners weren't happy with this. Wasn't there some way to get to the mine without using the wagon and get the drills? There was a back trail directly to the mine, up the ridge and across the shoulder of the mountain, but the only way to bring the heavy drills out would be to hook them each to one of the harness traces on one of the horses and drag them along, bouncing up and down on the rocks, careering down the hills. That would be okay; rock drills are tough anyway. So up through the fading light, soft snow drifting down, high up on the shoulder of the green mountain, we made our way through the pines to the old mine. A spooky place, abandoned years ago without bothering to take out the diesel engine, compressor, drills, and a lot of other equipment. We hooked one of the drills to each horse and started back down the mountain. Dark set in and snow began, big heavy wet white flakes, not quite a blizzard, but not reassuring.

By the time we got to the canyon and the wagon it was pitch dark, and time for the strenuous work of getting the wagon, locked into the rocks in the big pine grove, apart and back together facing the other way. We should have done it before going up the mountain, but the miners had been in a hurry. Now it had to be done in the dark. The miners wanted to build a fire and get warm, but I argued that things were getting tight and it was time to work hard and get the hell out of there. They refused and went ahead building a fire, saying that they had hired me and the wagon and it was my problem to get them back. Angry enough to be able to do it, I got the box out of the bolsters onto a rock, took the reach out, reversed the wheels, and put the box back in.

They got in sullenly and hunched down in their coats. I couldn't see a thing and let the horses find the way. Fine until we came to a bridge they didn't like. They spooked, backed and snorted, the harness rattling and jangling, wouldn't go on. I got down and took hold of the leader's bridle and led them across the bridge. It seemed easier on foot, so I stayed walking, leading the horses and talking to them. About eleven at night we got back to the ranch. The miners went up to the cabin, and I took the horses to the barn.

By the time I had unharnessed and fed the horses, the miners and the woman were piling things in the car, saying they wanted to get out of there before the snow—by then about six inches deep—made it impossible to get up the steep hill that was the only way out of the canyon. That was fine with me, I had seen enough of them, but nothing was said about the ten dollars as they piled into the car. I was prepared to fight for it after the day just past. In fact, I was going to make it impossible for them to get out of there, and they must have felt the growing tension, for at the last minute they handed over an old dirty ten-dollar bill, got in the car, and roared out.

The next summer, after I was gone, they came back with an old Fordson tractor with a compressor on the back that they were taking up to the mine, planning to work it. They stopped to talk to my stepfather for a while, who learned then of what had happened the winter before, but when they got ready to go, the tractor, hand cranked, wouldn't start. They cranked it for a day and a half, taking turns, before it fired. Then they clanked out, and about a hundred yards up the road, broke the steering gear in a deep rut. There was a power reel on the front of the tractor with about a hundred feet of cable, and from there on—all the ten miles or so up that mountain, over those rocks to the mine—they reeled out the cable, fastened the end to a tree, then winched the tractor up by its own bootstraps, as it were, to the tree, where the same job began all over again.

These things merely emphasized what the miners had already taught me

The ranch on South Spring Creek, the week I left to join the navy. By March the snows had melted off the western canyon ridge, but they still lay deep in the bottom.

on that long, long earlier day about the futility of life lived with old broken-down equipment, about foolish ideas that have no chance of succeeding. In a world where disaster is always ready to happen, it is best to look for something that has a chance of working.

Seventeen years old, a few months out of high school, no job, there was only one thing I knew to do, what all inland mountain boys do, go to sea. I think my parents were glad to see me go; one less pair of hands, but also one less mouth to feed, one less worry about what was going to happen. They were a little ashamed of not having been able to send me to college or to provide a living for me, but nobody had helped them out, and they were, I thought, glad I had relieved them of their vague feelings of guilt and responsibility.

And so one day in March, with heavy snow clouds hanging gray over the ranch, I borrowed ten dollars—having long ago spent my profits from the trip to the mine—and got a ride down to Cheyenne. A ground blizzard was blowing on U.S. 30 from Rawlins to Cheyenne. Blazing bright sunlight and blue sky above, snow blowing a few inches above the ground so thickly that it was impossible to see the road. The markers along the roadside were the only guides, and the swirling snow on the ground disoriented you.

I found the recruiting center in the post office and signed up for a minority enlistment—until I was twenty-one years old—in the United States Navy.

The train from Cheyenne went down to Denver in the evening. There, in a room in Union Station, about a hundred young men were assembled from all over the Rocky Mountains to take the oath. Everyone was young—seventeen, eighteen, nineteen—for the most part, kids who couldn't get jobs. Here and there were men in their twenties, jobless workers at the end of their rope, or incorrigible "fuck-ups" who had gotten into some kind of trouble at home and had been given the ancient choice by the judge of going to jail or joining one of the services. Most were from small towns, usually from broken families, notable for bad teeth and bad complexions, the marginal American young produced by more than ten years of the hardest of times.

After the oath we went out to the cold platform and into the warm cars. Not expecting much, we murmured our pleasure at the sleeping berths the navy provided its newest members, as if to say what I always found the navy to say, that it cared and provided well for those who served it.

The long yellow Union Pacific train, with its streamlined engine and coaches, snaked down in long curves out of Colorado and New Mexico, across the mountains and off the high central plateau to stop in the bright sunshine of California on the second morning. The warmth itself was luxurious after the cold of the mountains, and the orange groves and Spanish architecture had the look of freedom and pleasure found after a long search for a way out. Los Angeles only glimpsed, Union Station, and then the train went around a bend and there was the Pacific Ocean, blue and infinite, the place of adventure and excitement, stretching out to the horizon and beyond, Hawaii, the Philippines, Indonesia, China, and Japan. I would see them all, I was sure, and in time I did, but not quite as I imagined them in that moment of wild surmise.

TWO

Boots

The United States Naval Training Station, San Diego, was in 1941 the boot camp for all those who enlisted in the mountain region and the West Coast. Stuck out, next to the marine boot camp, on an arm of land extending in a westerly curve to Point Loma, forming the northwestern shore of San Diego Bay, the camp faced the Naval Air Station on North Island, across the water. The huge harbor and its shores were the training center for the Pacific Fleet. Inside the main gate of the training station, two-story stucco barracks, with arcades stretched out in long rows to the blacktop "grinder," the drill field where we would spend most of the next few months learning the naval axiom that military duties take precedence over trade skills by marching as a company under arms back and forth, up and down, on the oblique, to the rear, rear, rear, harch!

California had a sweet almost primitive quality, with its soft warm air, light breezes, and the lift that intense unremitting sunlight gives. The climate had a holiday air even in those strenuous first days, which began with a physical exam where the city boys laughed at those of us from the country still wearing long underwear. Since my long johns came only to the waist, with a T-shirt above, I thought myself quite sophisticated, but this was still far from the West Coast jockey-short high style, and blushing with embarrassment I was glad to package the underwear with my other clothes—the Hart, Schafner and Marx suit bought as a high school graduation present, my stepfather's cut-down coat, the gray hat—to be sent home. Civilian identity vanished with the clothes, and naked, we were initiated into our new identities, which were minimal, by probing, poking, testing, shooting. The barbers sheared off almost all our hair, leaving only an inch on top, bare on the sides. For some the loss of long, carefully groomed hair was as painful as it was to Samson, but to most it was only a necessary part of becoming a sailor.

Once out of the barbershop, we counted off, and when the number reached one hundred, two chief petty officers advanced purposefully and claimed us as a company. Chief Dahlgren was a gunner's mate, tall, tolerant, composed, Nordic. Chief Bilbo was short, stocky, fiery, and truly dangerous to disappoint. Company 41-39 was the 39th company formed at San Diego in 1941, and after being assigned a barracks, it was marched off to stores, where the navy issued the clothes and equipment needed to live in and work with from then on.

Whap! the heavy canvas hammock landed on the red brightly polished linoleum deck (no longer a floor) in front of each man, who then dragged it along in front of the counters where endless items were called out—"Two undress uniforms, white, one pair of high shoes, black"—and thrown on the hammock. Seabag for all clothing, ditty bag for toilet gear and personal possessions. Dress blues (1) with a white stripe around the right shoulder to identify you as a deckhand, not a red-striped engineer, and one white tape around the cuffs to mark you as the lowest of all ranks in the navy, an apprentice seaman. Black silk neckerchiefs (2) to be folded into a long flat ribbon and tied around the neck with a square knot exactly at the bottom of the vee in the blouse. Undress blues, no tape on collar and uncuffed sleeves; undress whites, dress whites no longer being issued; dungarees for work details; white caps and blue wool flat cap; peacoat (to be paid for later); one pair of low dress shoes.

The pile on the hammock grew mountainous: smallclothes (underwear), line for lashing up the hammock, cord for hanging clothes up to dry, a flat mattress and two covers, pillow, shoe brush and dauber, socks, black and white. At the end of the line two sailors grabbed the hammock, folded it double, put the rings on either end in your hand, and hoisted it onto your back. Bent double with this huge white hump on your back, you followed the arrows chalked on the sidewalk with your company number to the barracks where you were assigned a double-deck bunk and began to store your clothing in your seabag.

There was little personal gear. The navy did not encourage private possessions. A pocketknife was allowed, scissors, toothbrush and razor, soap, shoe polish, and some writing materials. These were kept in the ditty bag tied to the side of your bunk. There wasn't room for anything else, and no place elsewhere to stow anything. In time, on shipboard the seabag and ditty bag gave way to a small locker, but the Old Navy tradition of small ships and tight quarters hung on even there. It was most evident in the rigorous way in which the clothing was folded and stored. Each piece, from jumpers to skivvies, was folded in a particular way, rolled tightly, then tied with white cord, square knotted at a prescribed point, the cord ending in a brass collar just at the knot. No Irish pennants allowed here. The folds for storage gave the uniforms their distinctive appearance, like the three ridges on the collar of the blue and the white jumpers.

No dirt. Cleanliness was not next to godliness in the United States Navy, it was godliness. Everything in the barracks was constantly shined to a high gloss, from the red linoleum floors to the brasswork on the fire hose fittings. Shoes were a brilliant deep black in contrast with the unspotted white uniforms that were scrubbed every day with a stiff brush and harsh soap on the cement platforms provided for that purpose in the rear of the barracks. Men were expected to be as clean as their quarters and equipment, and most were so by easy choice.

Company 41-39 contained one of those odd people encountered here and there in every walk of life who not only smell foul after even a little exercise, but who nurture the smell by keeping themselves and their clothes as dirty as possible. Pigpen in the comic strip "Peanuts" is a mild version of this human oddity. Our Pigpen stuffed his seabag with dirty clothes, never brushed his teeth or washed, and lay in his bunk with one hand under the blanket (forbidden by unwritten rule), giggling, reading a comic book. The remedy was gleeful and brutal. From time to time he was stripped and put in the wash trough, surrounded by jeering recruits, secure in their own cleanliness, who washed him down with a gritty sand soap and then scrubbed him with long-handled brushes. The process, which involved a lot of hitting with the brush handles, was painful, a form of running the gauntlet, but it never had the slightest effect. When I last saw Pigpen he was lying in his bunk, smelling horrible, one hand under the blanket, giggling and reading the same page of the comic book he had been looking at when I first staggered into the barracks under my load of equipment. I thought then that he must always have been there, and he probably still is, some old Adam who haunts all efforts at cleanliness, positive thinking, and order.

We were children still, astonishingly stoical, self-reliant, tough children, but children still, and like all children, fascinated with killing. The guns drew us like magnets, and they gave them to us one afternoon in the huge cool armory, filled with the odor of Cosmoline, where each of us was issued and signed our life away for a rifle. Stands of boarding cutlasses still stood next to the cases of rifles, and so innocent were we that we thought boarding enemy vessels—just like Errol Flynn in the movies on the Spanish Main—was still a part of naval warfare and were disappointed when we had to be satisfied with only a murderous 16-inch bayonet.

Springfield rifles, 1903, .30 caliber, were the standard issue, but every seventh unlucky company, and the lot fell on 41-39, was given British-made long Enfields from the First World War. The Enfield weighed three pounds more than the Springfield, and we soon found out just what those three pounds meant at the end of a long, hot ten hours on the grinder. Not only that, you lived with that damned rifle in boot camp, using it in morning calisthenics, running around the grinder with it at high port for punishment, slamming it about your head and shoulder with one hand while going through the manual of arms. In the end you were stronger for having lugged that extra three pounds about with you, but Atlas could have been no gladder to get rid of his load than we were when we finally gave those huge heavy things back to the armorer.

The grinder was where the really hard lesson of military life, to put your individuality in storage and move as a group, was learned. Ten or more acres of baking black asphalt, shimmering with heat waves in the hot afternoon sun of the Mexican border. Here the company moved as a unit—white hats turned down to protect nose and neck from sunburn—five days a week, inspection on Saturday, up and down, by the right flank, by the left flank, to the rear, *march!* Eyes right, eyes left, eyes front, right shoulder arms, left shoulder arms. In four columns, tallest men at front. Blessed were the shortest for no one marched behind them to get out of step and scrape their well-polished heels with the toes of his shoes. Not only was it infuriating, hot and near exhaustion, to be stepped on by some bastard who couldn't keep step—and there were those congenitally unable to do so—but it also scuffed the backs of the shoes, making it impossible to polish them smoothly and deeply again, which led to trouble at the next inspection. Reasonable excuses were not a part of this life.

The company would be moving smoothly along, the Olympian Dahlgren at front swinging a sword on his shoulder, Bilbo at the rear, shouting time, "Hut, two, three, four, and your left, your right, your left, goddammit!" Then a shout, "You dirty son of a bitch," and turmoil would break out in the middle of the ranks, a few blows. Someone had still, once again, stepped on somebody's heels "for the last time." The company would halt, order would be restored, punishments handed out, and off we would go, "Your left, your right, your left, hold up your fucking heads."

After fifty years, the only name I remember from this group with whom I lived so intimately for months is one Mudrick, who marched immediately behind me, had trouble keeping step, whined a lot, and filled my heart with red murder on those blazing afternoons when he stepped on my heels again and again and snickered when I grumbled. Years later there was a cross-grained literary critic named Marvin Mudrick, whom I never knew, but whom I loathed on the unlikely suspicion that it must be the same man, up to his old trick of being out of step.

Money was no problem because we had none. The few coins that everyone hoarded were saved for cigarettes—it was a part of manhood to smoke at that time—which could be bought during a once-weekly few minutes in the ship's store at the duty-free price of five cents a package. There was no time to smoke during the day, and the smoking lamp was always out in the barracks. But during the evening while washing clothes the fortunate few with cigarettes could light up. Their pleasure was lessened a great deal by the envious faces that gathered around watching them as intently as begging dogs. As soon as they took the cigarette pack out of the sleeve of the skivvy shirt, where it was rolled up in the material to keep the cigarettes from being sweated on, a loud cry of "butts" would come from the throat of some wretch whose need for nicotine had overwhelmed self-control. The cry was privileged, and as soon as the first smoker had smoked his fill, he had to turn over the butt to the man who had claimed it rather than putting it in the sand bucket provided for that purpose. Usually the man who had been "butted" couldn't take the hungry look of the "butter," and so he smoked the cigarette down only halfway before giving up angrily in disgust. As time passed and fewer had cigarettes, the sound of "butts" would be followed by the desperate call of "butts on the butts!" "Butts on the butts on the butts" was only a joke, but there were those who would have tried it if social opinion would have tolerated it.

"Twenty-one dollars a day, once a month" was the refrain of an old song, and twenty-one dollars a month was the pay of recruits, or apprentice seamen, to use the official rank. The navy didn't bother paying at the end of the first month in boot camp on the theory that you had no need of money since you couldn't go on liberty until the end of the second month. But at the end of the second month the solemn naval ritual of payday began with the posting of the pay lists a few days before payday. All to be paid were on the list with first, second, and third names. If you lacked a middle name, the navy, sure that all humans needed a middle name for purposes of identification, supplied one, namely, "None." None was the most frequent middle name in the navy, and Samuel None Jones or Fred None Smith would be followed by the amount the navy figured it owed you after all deductions were made.

The amount was always less than the sailor calculated he had coming to him. This was why the lists were posted beforehand, so that the arguments could be sorted out before you passed, neatly dressed in the uniform of the day, in alphabetical order down the line before the yeomen and that august figure, the warrant paymaster. If you were going home on leave after boot camp, money was saved to pay for your train ticket; payments had to be made on the heavy peacoat, which was bought on time; any fines or punishments were deducted. And then, at the end of the line, looking particularly grim, Bilbo and Dahlgren were standing behind the Red Cross and the Navy Relief representatives, each of whom had to be given a dollar if you wanted to avoid getting on the company's permanent shitlist, which brought all kinds of drab extra work. Lifelong dislikes of the Red Cross were born in front of the superior looking, elegantly uniformed lady who disdainfully took your dollar while chatting with one of the supervising officers. But Navy Relief, which provided for families of enlisted men fallen on hard times, though burdensome, was accepted as a part of life. The families of enlisted men in peacetime had an Appalachian quality about them at best, so grim as to make everyone both sorry for them and determined to avoid marriage and children at all costs.

There were always navy ships in San Diego harbor, and on the first liberty, Saturday from noon to ten o'clock, they drew me, along with many others, across the bay to the North Island docks to spend a fireman's holiday going from one great ship to another. The aircraft carrier *Lexington*, a block long and tall as a hotel, was irresistible. We asked the officer-of-the-deck permission to come aboard—"Permission granted"—and saluted toward the rear of the ship, where the flag was flown at anchor, in the manner we had been instructed. With a few smiles at our oversize boot uniforms and rounded hats we were allowed to wander about looking at the planes on the hangar deck, the guns small and large alongside the immense flight deck. The high smokestack with ladder rungs welded on the side was so tempting that I climbed up to near the top, getting more and more frightened at the height, until someone called from below telling me to get the hell off.

The streetcar clanged back to "Dago" where the streets were filled with sailors on liberty; the bars, with someone sitting on a stool at each door to examine your liberty card to make sure you were twenty-one, stood with their doors open and the jukeboxes blaring out "Hut sut rawson on the rilli-raw" and "Drinking rum and coca cola, Working for the Yankee dollar." Neon lights flashed over "The Arabian Palace Hotel" and "Intimate Nights," where the Shore Patrol stood on the sidewalks swinging their clubs and looking mean. People you knew were in the tattoo parlors actually getting dragons, daggers, and "Death before Dishonor" inscribed on their arms and backs, the bright inks mixed with sweat and blood standing in pools.

Of all the walkers on the streets, only the boots with floppy white issue uniforms and broad white hats sitting squarely on the head and flaring straight out, neckerchiefs tied at the vee of the jumper rather than at the throat, looked like the real rubes. Everyone else looked in the know, tight uniforms, campaign ribbons, old chief boatswains' mates from the Asiatic station, and long-term hands with rows of gold hash marks. It was an enlisted man's world on the streets, the officers, unenvied, stayed with their stylish but strained-looking women in their club in Coronado or in one of the good hotels.

There was real vulgar joy among so much life. An entire symbology of hierarchy and skill, avidly and quickly learned, flashed along the streets. A red stripe around the left shoulder for below-deck firemen, white around the right for seamen deckhands. Petty officers with rating badges on the left arm for the trades, on the right for those who worked on deck like quartermasters, gunners, and coxswains. Red hash marks on the lower arm, one for every four years of service; gold hash marks after twelve years. White uniforms, dress blues, khakis and greens here and there on the aviation chiefs. Lots of sailors were in "civvies," usually a garish Hawaiian or a Philippine shirt, with tight trousers and cheap boots that were kept, along with a bottle, in rented lockers in locker clubs where you could drink, shower, and change clothes for liberty. Selling uniforms and badges was big business. Outside each store an affable man called out "Hey, chief!" to the boots as they walked along, trying to lure them into buying tight-fitting tailor-made uniforms, silk lined, gold dragons stitched into the lining of the panel above the crotch. "Liberty" was, I felt at once, the right word for it.

In time basic training ended, and those who were going straight to the fleet without further training to become deckhands and firemen were given a ten-day leave, and with any luck had saved enough money to pay for a train ticket. The rest of us went off to another three months in a training school to learn a trade. It was necessary to pass some rudimentary exams to be accepted for one of the training schools. Since promotion supposedly came more rapidly to those with a trade, and the work was easier, schools were thought desirable. Besides, the great reason given for joining the navy in those Depression days was to learn a trade. But it wasn't anything so practical that directed my choice. Out of all the useful skills I could have learned—radio, electricity, mechanics, signaling, quartermastering, even boiler making—wild about flying and airplanes, I chose aviation ordnance, bombs, aerial torpedoes, machine guns, smoke laying, and other instruments of destruction. This was thought a good route to flying as a gunner or observer, even to pilot training.

With our seabags lashed up in our hammocks and all our belongings on our shoulders, looking like real seamen for the first time, we walked up the hill to the holding barracks for the long row of training schools. Here you were held until enough people arrived in your specialty to form a class, and in the meantime the navy found work for idle hands. The barracks were new and built about three feet off the ground on spaced cement pilings. Someone had had the idea that it would be good to fill the empty space with dirt dug from the clay hill behind the barracks. The dirt was loaded in wheelbarrows and then dumped in baskets that were dragged by hand, there not being room for the wheelbarrows under the buildings, to the center of the area, dumped, and pushed back.

It was dirty and hard work, and I was delighted when the chief in charge of the barracks selected me and one other young sailor to clean his room. The room was only about ten by six with a bunk, a chair, and a locker, and one person, let alone two, could have kept it spotless working about half an hour a day. Innocent as lambs, the other sailor and I never questioned our good fortune, slicking up the room, running a few errands, and then loafing in the ship's store or reading magazines in out-of-the-way areas. I don't think I had ever heard of homosexuality, and when the chief, having sent the other cleaner off on a pretext, made his smiling, good-natured move, I was so aghast that I jumped without thinking in one giant leap out of the open window, which fortunately was on the first floor.

No hard feelings, but within the hour I was back on the dirt gang with the worst job, at the front of the line, pushing the dirt by hand up tight under the barracks' floor. But in a few days the class for aviation ordnance school filled up, and we moved to another barracks, double-decker bunks along each side, with a long desk made of two planks, with fixed benches, running down the center for study. Light and clean, simple but efficient, it was a pleasant place to spend the late summer and fall of 1941. The course itself was ridiculously easy—a few simple facts about electricity and some rudimentary circuits, learning the difference between one type of bomb rack and another, some information about various explosives and the fuses used to ignite them, how to break down, clean, and adjust machine guns, pistols, rifles.

Probably the most complicated mechanism was the aerial torpedo, which ran on an ingenious little steam engine fired by alcohol and contained a lot of complex gyroscopes and settings to control depths and angles. Only at the Battle of Midway did I come to know that what seemed so marvelous a piece of technology was deeply flawed, seldom running true and regularly failing to explode. But at the time, it was presented, like all the fairly crude weaponry we worked on, as the latest martial technology, to be understood and cared for with skill and hard work.

We saw no real airplanes in training school; instead we bore-sighted machine guns (that is, aligned them to converge their fire at a certain number of yards in front of the plane) on a frame model. Learning on a mock-up to synchronize machine guns so that they could fire through a turning propeller without hitting the blades, we made a gambling game out of whether the firing solenoid clicked on empty space or on an old propeller turned slowly by hand.

For someone with a good memory and a feel for simple systems, it was all ridiculously easy, but for others, I learned, it was a slow drudgery, involving sitting up in the heads all night to try to get the facts down for one of the dreaded weekly exams. Many flunked out, but most passed, and all through the war I ran into them in odd places in the Pacific, filling practice bombs with sand, caring for ammunition storage depots, taking the temperatures in the bomb magazines of aircraft carriers, cleaning machine guns, and loading bombs.

If you kept out of trouble, the navy was a genial place, and at the training schools we found that ten- or twelve-hour liberties were given on three out of four weekends. On the fourth your section had the watch. By now we had become second-class seamen, with a pay raise from twenty-one to thirty-six dollars a month, which meant for the first time that we had actual money in hand after we were paid every two weeks. Everyone bought a small black wallet designed to tuck without much bulge into a uniform waistband.

Before the war the navy had the quaint custom of paying in two-dollar bills, perhaps because no one else would take them, but the sailors all said it was because two dollars was what was charged in the whorehouses in Dago.

In a small town crowded with sailors, life gravitated to the bars and the whore-houses. Eighteen-year-olds like myself, with little cash, were not very welcome in either, even with doctored identification, but no one really worried much, and sooner or later you could work your way into a bar to sit with your friends, eight or ten in a booth, and tell stories about what a good job you had had back in civilian life, how much money you made, your flashy clothes and car, the adoring and obliging girlfriends. Having had none of these I listened happily to the more polished liars, kept time to the music of the jukebox, and basked in the sense of being one of a group of real men of the world.

The local beer was the drink, cheap and sufficient for inexperienced drinkers like myself, but sometimes money would be pooled to buy a pint of some bright-colored gin—sloe, mint, apricot—more memorable for its vividness coming up than the pleasure it gave going down, and with this in a paper bag we would sit on the curb, or sometimes, five or six together, take a room in one of the whorehouses. Some quirk of the law required them actually to rent rooms, which they did for a few dollars, and groups of sailors would take one to sit drinking in and talking to the whores, strongly perfumed, who came in from time to time for a drink and to see if there was any business.

You could also sit in the parlors for a limited time looking at the girls in scanty costumes who displayed themselves provocatively, and then move on to another house, and another. It was all incredibly garish and tawdry; most people would probably think the strong sounds and smells vulgar, even disgusting, but to young men in their late teens, their experience of women limited for the most part to a few awkward pawings, their glands in an uproar and their sexual urgencies flowing full tide, it looked like Babylon itself, the harem of the sultans, the paradise of the true believers. The Oriental motif extended to a pale, slender young girl called Cleo, who with good humor and real tenderness took me through my sexual initiation on a sagging old bed in a quiet room, music faintly in the distance, and a cool breeze playing gently over our bodies from the electric fan. It was not a romantic setting, far from it—sensible and workmanlike, rather—but it was not brutal or degrading for anyone.

Later on the stairs going out I heard a drunken sailor who had gotten in an argument with a whore cursing the madam. She screamed back at him, "You want to hurt someone? You fucking cocksucker. Come on and fuck me, and I'll show you how to hurt someone fucking." This had nothing to do with me or the sex I knew, and I hurried on out to the bus back to the base where, after the liberty card was deposited in the box, reality spoke up again in the prophylactic station where you squirted some stinging brown liquid up your cock—sometimes fainting when you did so—washed, and used an antiseptic cream. Gonorrhea was endemic in the fleet, and fearful tales went around of syphilis picked up in the Orient, requiring long, painful treatment, spinal taps, and eventuating in various kinds of rot and disintegration.

But it was all soon finished. I was the honor man of the class, not because of any manual skills, I was a bit clumsy, but because of the written tests. The chief arranging graduation ceremonies had never laid eyes on me and did not know my name, so when he called it out to tell me to go up on the stage at the graduation, he had to ask someone, "Who is he?" A mark of great success to me and to my friends. You did your work and got ahead but remained totally anonymous. This is how you survived in the navy, and most other places in the world, before the triumph of the modern cult of personality.

At those graduation ceremonies on October 21, 1941, I shook hands for the first time with a real officer, creatures seen only from a distance theretofore. Capt. Henry Gearing was the commander of the United States Naval Training Station, San Diego, a grizzled old sea dog, at least in appearance, bluff, tall, commanding. When he saw me on the stage, small and thin and extremely young looking, he leaned over and whispered as he gave me the diploma, "My God, boy, how old are you?" I thought I had set his concerns entirely at ease by truthfully answering, "Eighteen," and went out to the tune of "Anchors Aweigh" to collect my gear and go off for fifteen days of leave at home in Wyoming.

Two days sitting up on a train so packed as not even to have any standing room left returned me to the cold of Wyoming. Rawlins, where the train stopped, is sixty miles from our ranch across the bleak desert of south-central Wyoming. Up in the mountains a few inches of snow had fallen already by the end of October, the yellow leaves were all gone from the aspens, and at the point where they ended and the green pines began the dark and cold of winter were already to be felt. The mountains rose up and up through the pines to the bare space above timberline. Their bald peaks dominated our ranch, loomed over everything with menacing size and durability. They set the scale of reality, of things as they permanently are, and against them everything else seemed ephemeral and puny. The new cabin with the stone fireplace, for the dudes who would never come, the ranch itself and all the hopes invested in it, the faraway sunniness of California, where nature seems to promise a lot, and even the might of the United States Navy were emptied of reality by those monstrous mountains and the oncoming winter. Even now, a half century later, when everything else seems to have changed, scarcely a rock has moved on those everlasting hills.

I had expected to return a hero, and the dog was glad to see me, and my mother fussed over me and listened with real interest to my stories. My step-father, who had avoided service in the First World War, felt somewhat threatened by my martial authority and constantly told me there wouldn't be a war. But it all seemed anticlimactic. My life and interests had trans-ferred elsewhere, and, half aware of it, I had some guilt for not feeling the old loyalty and interest. A brief trip to the small town, Saratoga, where nothing had happened since I left and no one was at all interested in my adventures, was oddly painful.

It was the last time I saw my mother alive, and as I write this, I am trou-bled how little I can remember of her, barely able to see her worried face in the lamplight or hear her words of good advice as I left. The big snows held off, and in early November 1941, they drove me back to the train that took me to the bustle of San Diego and on to Pearl Harbor.

THREE

Pearl

The USS *Procyon*, a military cargo vessel, sailed from San Diego to Pearl Harbor in mid-November 1941, loaded with various stores and machines and packed with sailors being sent out to the fleet, many of us recruits going overseas for the first time. The strictest seniority is the navy's governing rule, and what this means in a practical way is that all the dirty jobs that have to be done every day to keep things running fall to the newest and the lowliest in rank. My introduction to this came at once and in the classic way—"captain of the head." The moment I stepped aboard, I was assigned to keep spotless and shined to a high gloss the decks, the showers, the bulkheads, and the troughs of running seawater in one of the toilets. I craned my neck out of a porthole to see Point Loma, the dangling peninsula that protected San Diego harbor, known to generations of sailors as "Point Hard On" because of its shape and its effect on those returning from, not going on, long voyages overseas. Once around Point Loma and into blue water the ship began to pick up speed, and as she did, she began to pitch and roll in the usual way. But it was news to my stomach, never having been at sea before. I heaved for a while, and then groaned for a day or two while I swung the heavy swab cleaning the head, until my appetite came back and my sea legs set. I was never seasick again in my life.

Five days out we came in the early morning around Diamond Head and went down the shore opposite Honolulu, and then through the nets and buoys into the narrow entrance to Pearl Harbor, then the home port of the Pacific Fleet. The water formed a ring around Ford Island in the center of the anchorage, the Naval Air Station where the patrol squadrons of PBYs, the Catalina flying boats, were based and where the squadrons from the aircraft carriers operated while they were in port. The *Procyon* tied up in the navy yard, and immediately a swarm of motor whaleboats arrived to pick up the personnel assigned to the various ships and deliver them to their new homes. The air was electric with excitement, the tropical surroundings and soft smells, the huge and busy naval base, the ships of all kinds, long rows of battleships, aircraft carriers, submarines, cruisers, destroyers, minesweepers. If you were of a warlike turn of mind this was the place, fairly breathing the invincible power of the United States Navy.

I was fascinated with airplanes at that time, like so many others of my age, and it seemed to me a stroke of good luck beyond belief that I had been assigned to Torpedo Squadron Six, part of Air Group 6 on the USS *Enterprise* (CV 6), the newest of three carriers in the Pacific Fleet at that time, along with the older *Lexington* and *Saratoga*. The sister ship of the *Enterprise*, the USS *Yorktown* (CV 5), was on her way to the Pacific. The *Enterprise* was tied up on the western side of Ford Island taking on fuel and bombs, and as the motor whaleboat came up under her counter on her seaward, port, side, she towered a hundred feet above us, grayish white, nearly nine hundred feet long, beautifully shaped despite her huge size. The squadron was in barracks ashore with the planes, but I was assigned a bunk on ship and given an hour to wander around, staring with wonder at the complicated machinery, stowage spaces, elevators, and spare planes tied up in the overhead of the vast hangar deck. It was all so extraordinarily busy, the sailors in spotless white shorts and T-shirts rushing here and there—a crew of nearly two thousand—the public address system constantly blaring out bugle calls, the shrill of boatswain's whistles, and unintelligible orders to "hear this" or "hear that." It was a total and instant love affair with this great ship, never lost and never felt again in quite the same way for another.

Many years after the war in which the *Enterprise* became the most famous of American warships, she was about to be broken up, and there was a national campaign to raise money to save her as a museum. I thought about it but decided not to contribute because I couldn't bear to think of her sitting around in some backwater, being exploited in unworthy ways, invaded by hordes of tourists with no sense of her greatness. Better by far, I thought, to leave her to memory of those who had served on her when she was fully alive, vibrating under full steam at thirty-two knots, the aircraft turning up, guns firing, heeling over so sharply that the hangar deck took on water to avoid the bombs. Others must have felt the same way, for the funds fell short, and she went for scrap, to be succeeded by a huge nuclear carrier of the same name. Better that, I still think, than to be like the *Intrepid* in New York harbor, where the school groups clatter and squeal, the professional veterans come to be photographed, and the politicians make patriotic speeches on holidays.

I was brought down to earth by being put that afternoon on the anchor-chain chipping detail. Life on board ship is a constant battle with rust in which the weapons are the chipping hammer, the wire brush, red lead and gray paint. The anchor chain is particularly vulnerable to rust and in port is regularly taken out of the chain storage and laid out in a barge alongside, each huge link more than three feet in length. The trick is to take all the old paint off, wire brush the rust off down to bare pitted metal, put a priming coat of paint on, followed by two or three coats of regular paint. Hard work, dirty, tiring, hot, and totally unappreciated. The members of the air group, scornfully called "Airedales" by the rest of the crew, were normally exempt from this kind of scut work, but the real king of the ship, Jocko—a boatswain's mate first class, the ship's master-at-arms, a kind of chief of police cum ward politician—was happy to hold transfers like me in his transit group as long as possible, just to use them for such heavy jobs as this.

After a few days the ground crews of the air group came back aboard in preparation for sailing, and Murphy, the chief of the ordnance gang in the torpedo squadron, instantly reclaimed me on the familiar grounds that he was already shorthanded and needed every trained man he could get. The deck crews regarded this as a bushwa, just a plausible excuse, but the ship officially recognized that the airplanes were her primary armament and gave priority to their operation. I was overjoyed to be given a bunk in the squadron compartment, made known to the leading chief and the yeomen who kept the records, and, above all, given a place, however low, in the ordnance gang, which meant a coffee cup and a right to sit around in the ordnance shack, a wire-mesh enclosure suspended just below the flight deck, where our tools were kept. Here Murphy and his leading petty officer, Freddy Moyle, kept court, quietly and happily drunk on "moosemilk," a mixture of coffee and bombsight alcohol, of 99 percent purity, used for cleaning the Norden bombsights, the supply of which was fortuitously in Murph's charge.

Ordnancemen worked in pairs: an experienced petty officer and a striker, the navy's name for an apprentice, like myself, learning the ropes. Each pair had responsibility for three planes, seeing to it that the guns were kept clean and adjusted, the bomb racks working, the torpedo gear in good shape, and so on. Most of the work was more communal, involving all the ordnance gang, belting ammunition, bringing bombs up from the magazine and fusing them, hauling the torpedoes out on long hydraulic trucks to the planes and loading them, changing bomb racks so that different weights of bombs could be carried. It was simple work but required a lot of running about and a lot of dexterity and sure movements, which came only with practice.

The torpedo squadron of eighteen planes at full complement, which seldom happened, was one of four making up the air group. Besides the "fish" there were two identical squadrons of eighteen dive-bombers, one specializing in scouting, VS-6, and one in dive-bombing, VB-6. Providing cover for the ship and protection for the torpedo planes and bombers was a squadron of eighteen fighter planes, VF-6. Among them these seventy-two planes were supposed to be able to deliver a coordinated attack against any naval target, the fighters flying protection overhead, the dive-bombers going in first from high altitude, followed at sea level by the torpedo planes to deliver the coup to the enemy ships. To me, with my modest conceptions of warfare, it all looked like the most up-to-date and modern technology, Buck Rogers himself. But it was, of course, woefully inadequate for the battles to come, and the officers who flew in the squadrons and ran the ships were as naive about their equipment and tactics as I was.

The torpedo plane came from the middle 1930s. The TBD, translated "torpedo bomber, made by Douglas Aircraft," was totally obsolete. Designed to carry three men—pilot, observer-bomber in the center, and radioman gunner in the rear—it could do only about a hundred knots with a torpedo, a fatally slow speed for escaping shipboard antiaircraft gunners and fast fighter planes. It was not much faster with a load of four five-hundred-pound bombs, or eight one-hundred-pounders, and used with bombs as a high-level bomber with the Norden bombsight, it was both inaccurate and a sitting duck. Defensively it was ludicrous: one .30-caliber fixed machine gun synchronized to fire forward through the propeller and one free .30 caliber in the rear fired by the radioman. Later there were two guns in the rear, but the increase in firepower was offset by the awkwardness of handling their weight. About all you could say about it positively was that with its huge wingspan and light weight, it seldom crashed, and it floated onto the deck at a nice, slow landing speed.

But to me it looked like some spaceship bound for Mars, and I polished up all the ordnance gear on my planes daily, disassembled the guns down to the smallest parts, cleaned them, and adjusted the headspace far more often than was needed.

The demand for labor of the most basic kind was endless on board ship, and the first year or two in the fleet was usually spent going from one of these menial jobs to another. The squadron had to supply men to the plane-handling crews, and as the newest arrival in the squadron, and therefore the lowest in the pecking order, I was soon off to a life that was healthy but in many respects like a chain gang. My days from before dawn until after dark were spent on the flight deck, wearing a dark blue T-shirt and a canvas helmet dyed the same color, buckled tightly under the chin, pushing the planes at a dead run back and forth. When planes were landing, all those on board had to be pushed forward to leave room at the rear of the flight deck. Those for which there was no space were pushed onto one of the three elevators and taken down to the hangar deck where other crews picked them up and moved them around the hangar deck.

There were always too many planes for the room available on the two decks, and they had to be spotted with the greatest skill. When planes were taking off, the process was reversed, with all the planes to be launched spotted aft on the flight deck with clear space in front of them. Then, as the ship turned into the wind and went to flank speed, to provide the greatest possible airspeed, the plane being launched went to full power with the brakes on, released them suddenly, and used the combination of its forward speed and the wind to, usually, lift it into the air by the time it reached the forward end of the deck.

As soon as the planes were off, the blue plane-handlers leaped out of the catwalks where we had been waiting and began to respot the deck for planes coming in to land. In the days before tractors to pull the planes, all of this complicated maneuvering was done entirely by muscle power. Since the effectiveness of the carrier depended on the speed and efficiency with which it moved its planes about for launching and landing, and keeping the deck ready as much as possible to launch an attack, this was a high-pressured business, with a lot of shouting and running all day long, a lot like athletic teams. Except for lunch, you never left the deck from the time flight operations began before light until their end after dark, and any moment of rest was passed sitting at the side of the island, asleep in an instant, usually, so that you were there immediately if needed. Lots of military drills are more pretense than reality, but this one was in dead earnest, and in the coming war, battles were lost and won by the plane-handling on the carriers. The Japanese lost the Battle of Midway because of a failure to handle their planes properly.

The *Enterprise* left Pearl Harbor at the end of November loaded, along with her own air group, with the fighter planes of a marine squadron that was to be taken to Wake Island and flown off to the coral landing strip there. Wake was the closest of our bases to Japan and an ominous place, as the grim faces of the pilots showed when they flew off to the island. In a few weeks they were all dead, along with a boy named Bobby Mitwalsky, who had gone to school with me and joined the marines when I went into the navy. I remembered him most for a leather jacket he had with panels of admirable blue fur.

The clouds were heavy all the way back from Wake, and the storms continuous, the deck twisting down and to the side, waves breaking over the flight deck. The other ships in the task force, cruisers and destroyers, began to make heavy going of it, and the task force slowed down, delaying its entrance into Pearl Harbor from the night of December 6 to some time in the day of the seventh. Whenever the *Enterprise* went into port, since she could not launch or land aircraft while tied up, the planes were flown off to be land based so long as we were in harbor.

Early in the morning of the seventh our air group took off for Ford Island. The ship was empty without planes, and everyone was getting ready for docking in Berth 1010 alongside the navy yard, the starboard watch going ashore for liberty. But before nine o'clock, general quarters was sounded—a clanging bell followed by a stirring bugle call and a stern voice ordering, "All hands man your battle stations"—at the sound of which all hell broke loose, and thousands of sailors ran to the places all over the ship where they were assigned in battle. You had to run up ladders and down passageways, since as soon as possible after general quarters sounded, all watertight doors and hatches began to be closed and dogged down. No one was surprised at going to general quarters—submarine scares were common—but this was different. A huge battle flag was broken out and streamed out halfway down the deck from the yard. The captain came on the public address system to announce that Pearl Harbor had been bombed and that we were now at war with the Japanese. This was followed by reading the "Articles of War," a long list, as nearly as I could tell, of the reasons for which the navy could imprison you for life or shoot you. It certainly spoke of no rewards.

I didn't think of being killed, but I did wonder how long I was going to have to spend in the navy now. We were all apolitical then, disliking the Japanese and the Germans in a general kind of way, but not really knowing much about them. I could remember the evening with the sun going down on September 1, 1939, when my mother, stepfather, and I listened to the news on an old radio powered by a car battery and learned that Hitler had invaded Poland, and that Britain and France had declared war. We knew, sadly, far away though it was, that it would affect us, and that life would never again be the same. But I never read a newspaper, not even the daily mimeographed sheet put out aboard ship with ball scores and a few headlines, and knew nothing of how close we were to war. I knew vaguely that the Japanese had invaded China long ago and were still fighting there. Everyone knew the Japanese hated us, even as we despised them, and the old salts told stories of Japanese crews shouting at them, "Yankee, we sink you," when they passed in port.

So it was no surprise, somehow expected and taken for granted for a long time, though the reasons were beyond us. The ship stayed at general quarters; we were only a few miles south of the entrance to Pearl Harbor, and the scuttlebutt (named after the water cask on the old ships where sailors getting a drink of water exchanged gossip) began to circulate about the Japanese landing on Oahu, taking San Francisco, and on and on. Rumor is a remarkable thing, a really free play of the fearful imagination, but the truth was that after two air strikes the Japanese planes went back to their carriers north of Oahu, which turned at high speed and went back to ports I would see only four years and some later. We looked for the Japanese fleet and fortunately never found them, for, though some of our planes had returned to the ship—others had gotten mixed up in the battle and been shot down—a single carrier would have been no match for the enemy's six carriers.

Fuel was short in all the ships in the task force, and we had to go into port in the late afternoon of December 8, fueling at night and being a few miles at sea by dawn. Rumors of new attacks were everywhere, and since no one knew where the attack had come from, there was continued fear that it might come again. Everyone was keyed up, the ship was still at general quarters, which meant that I was on the flight deck where I could see everything in the fading light. The smell came first as we moved slowly through the nets guarding the channel, of fuel oil, burned paint and canvas, hot steel. Fires were still burning everywhere, and a heavy cloud of smoke hung over everything that had looked so bright and lively a week earlier. It was eerie, the huge ship moving painstakingly slowly through what was always a narrow channel into the harbor, made now much narrower by a battleship half on the mud on the port side, its stern sticking well out into the channel. The *Nevada* had managed to get under way during the attack but was hit again by torpedoes going out of the channel where she could not maneuver. The captain, realizing that his ship sunk in the channel would block the entire fleet, beached her on the Ewa side, leaving just enough room for the big carriers and their escorts, which was all that was left of the Pacific Fleet, to maneuver around him at painfully slow speed.

Sailors lined the shore everywhere to watch us and raise a few cheers for one of the last working ships in the Pacific Fleet. After inching around the battleship—oh, how slow it was when all we wanted to do was to get it over with and get out of there—the ship turned gradually a few points to starboard and started down the anchorage between battleship row to port and the dockyard and submarine base to starboard. At dock number 1010 in the yard, only a few hundred feet away, the minesweeper *Ogallala* was down, hit by three torpedoes that were intended for the *Enterprise* and would have been put into her, along with God knows how many bombs, if we had not been delayed by the storms. The Japanese, we learned later, had expected us to be there and had delivered the goods directly to the designated spot, even if there were only a few small ships where their maps showed an aircraft carrier.

It was on the port side, however, that the real devastation was visible, beginning with wrecked hangars and seaplanes on the tip of Ford Island. There, one after another—broken in two, turned over, canted crazily, under water with only the upper masts showing, burned, smoking and smoldering—was the long row of battleships, two by two, that everyone thought of as the main force of the Pacific Fleet and of the U.S. Navy. But in a violent way the attack had underlined that the day of the battleship was long gone, that it had been replaced by aircraft carriers like the one that was now picking her way daintily, almost disdainfully, down the harbor past the smoking hulks of the old navy devastated by planes from other foreign aircraft carriers.

The symbolism went even further, for the carrier-based Japanese planes not only sank the American battleships that day, they sank at the same time all those huge Japanese battleships that Admiral Yamamoto had brought with him from Japan to back up the carriers that delivered the attack. In a few days the Japanese would drive the lesson home still more forcefully on the other side of the Pacific Ocean when they would sink the British battleships *Prince of Wales* and *Repulse* under way, not tied up, with aircraft off Malaya.

Pearl Harbor seemed a terrible blow at the time, but it made no difference in the war to be fought, in which big-gunned battleships would only rarely fire their guns against one another; in which, again and again, surface vessels would be pounded and sunk by planes carrying bombs and torpedoes.

But this strategic irony was as far from the thoughts of the admiral commanding as it was from the mind of a raw recruit like myself. The moment itself was everything. Having been overwhelmed by all this mighty power so shortly before, I was now stunned, and more than a little frightened, by this sudden reversal that revealed the complete vulnerability and helplessness of these oil-sweating behemoths. There was no question of losing the war, but how would we win it? Surely not with a few aircraft carriers like the *Enterprise*, but there wasn't anything else.

One dreary scene succeeded another, and as night fell and we inched in slow motion around the northern end of Ford Island, guns went off here and there and machine-gun tracers filled the air from time to time as nervous gunners let loose at their fears. Then, to port, we passed the old target battleship *Utah*, with her bottom turned up to the sky, and just beyond her we tied up. The fuel lines came aboard in an instant, and all hands that could be spared from battle stations, which included me, formed lines from the magazines down the gangways onto Ford Island to pass into the ship the bombs and ammunition that were waiting there at the magazines to give us a full wartime supply of munitions. Food too came aboard in a rush, and a few extra crew, but not much else.

Each sailor was given two postcards to send home with a choice of two printed messages: "I am well and will write soon" or "I am wounded and will write details as soon as possible." At this point something fatal for me was put in train. Two cards meant one for the family and one for the girlfriend all sailors claimed to have. I did not have a girlfriend, wasn't even sure I wanted one, but you had to live up to the heroic moment, which required a girlfriend, so I sent my second card off to a girl in Saratoga I much admired but who was more than a little indifferent to me. Somehow the cards got separated in transit, and the card to the girl arrived first, while the one to my family was much delayed. By the time the first card arrived the ranch was snowed in, but someone trudged the five miles through the snow to tell my parents I was safe. My mother was relieved, but, in a disturbed state of mind from my departure and the beginning of the war, she conceived that I no longer cared for her and had transferred my loyalties to the girl, whom she didn't like. She concluded that I had had only one card and had used it for this purpose, and when her card arrived a week or two later, it made no difference in her feelings about my disloyalty.

By three or four in the morning the ship was loaded, many of the supplies still on the hangar deck waiting to be stowed below. The lines were cast off, and the *Enterprise* began to edge her way out the harbor, down the channel, through the nets, and into the blue water, picking up speed as she went, the sun rising, the water beginning to hiss alongside, and the smell of burning oil, charred paint, bodies, and defeat left far behind. The planes came aboard and the war had begun.

FOUR

Cruising

To a young man war is exciting, and there can have been few wars as excit-ing, at least at the start, as the naval war between the United States and Japan from December 1941 to September 1945. The ocean itself was vast and filled with mysterious places whose exotic names now became as famil-iar as the little towns in Wyoming where I had grown up had once been: Medicine Bow, Saratoga, Rawlins, Encampment, and Laramie. Now the names were Truk (the major Japanese base in the Marianas), Cavite and Bataan, the Java Sea and the Coral Sea, Guam and Wake Island, Mindanao and Balikpapan, New Caledonia and Guadalcanal.

Great fleets steamed across vast spaces of ocean at high speed, surprising the enemy with sudden raids and then disappearing into the emptiness of blue ocean extending from the Aleutians and the Bering Strait in the north to Port Moresby and New Zealand in the south, from the California coast to the Indian Ocean. The ships were fast, heavily armed, and technically con-siderably advanced, never before tried in combat, but now about to develop by trial and error a new kind of war of aircraft carriers, ship-based aircraft fighting with other ship-based aircraft for control of the air and the sea.

The crews on both sides at that point in the war were professional and volunteer; everyone was there because he had wanted, or at least agreed, to be there, and as a consequence the morale was high, as were the skills of the combatants. Few civilians were caught in the middle until we came to east Asia. It was a war both navies wanted, and, tired of messing with one another, they went at it with a lot of energy. We despised the Japanese at first, and it took a long time and a lot of pain to realize that, at least at the beginning of the war, theirs was a better navy than ours: better ships and air-craft, better-trained personnel, better tactics and fighting ability. We improved rapidly, but in the end we only overcame them by the sheer weight of equipment and men. They remained to the end a worthy foe—courageous, skilled, tenacious, gallant in their strange way—whom we had seriously underestimated. Never after the first days of the war did the fleet look down on "the Japs" or speak contemptuously, like the yellow press, of the cowardice of the enemy.

All of us on the *Enterprise* assumed after Pearl Harbor that she and the other carriers in the Pacific would be sent at once to relieve the Philippines, or at least to break up the attack on Wake Island. Our admiral, William F. "Bull" Halsey, a real fire-eater, thought so too. His quarters were just down the passageway, beneath the flight deck and the island, from our ordnance shack, and when we went down to try to wheedle fresh fruit from his mess attendants, we could hear him thundering away, cursing Washington and the shore-based admirals for their cowardice. The only reason we could think of for not being sent to sink the Japanese fleet forthwith—this is how we thought in our innocence—was that nearly all our battleships were lying broken and burned on the mud bottom of the anchorages alongside Ford Island.

But Adm. Chester Nimitz, soon to be the commander of the Pacific Fleet, must have had some understanding of what had happened at Pearl Harbor, for, as I learned many years later, when he was assembling the fleet to fight the Battle of Midway, he did not include the several seaworthy battleships that had at that time been assembled in San Francisco.

Wisely, no one ordered us to fight our way to Manila, Truk, or Yokosuka, and we were kept on patrols during December and early January, guarding the approaches to the Hawaiian Islands, going back and forth across the 180th meridian, the International Date Line. On December 24, 1941, with a kind of black humor, we crossed the dateline to the west at midnight, so that it became December 25, and then crossed back on the twenty-sixth, getting two Christmases that way, neither very joyful.

The American carriers—there were still only three, *Lexington*, *Yorktown*, and *Enterprise*, after the *Saratoga* was hit by a torpedo in early January—operated separately, each the center of a task force. Cruising the ocean with one carrier in the middle of a task force of a few heavy cruisers and destroyers soon became routine. Standard watches were Condition Three—four hours on duty and eight off—and Condition Two—four hours on and four off—with most watertight doors and hatches dogged closed. It was difficult to move about the ship under these conditions, and everyone was always tired. Reveille came before sunrise so that general quarters could be sounded in time for everyone to be at their battle stations at sunrise. Sunrise and sun-

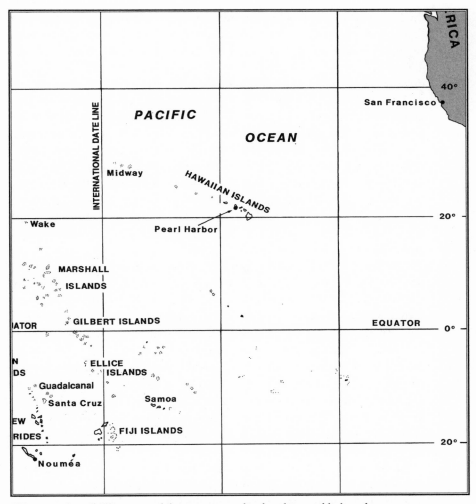

PACIFIC

OCEAN

San Francisco

40°

INTERNATIONAL DATE LINE

Midway

HAWAIIAN ISLANDS

Pearl Harbor

20°

Wake

MARSHALL
ISLANDS

GILBERT ISLANDS

IATOR

EQUATOR

0°

N
DS

ELLICE
ISLANDS

Guadalcanal
Santa Cruz

Samoa

EW
RIDES

FIJI ISLANDS

20°

Nouméa

We cruised in the first year of the war across the date line and below the equator.

set were considered the two most dangerous moments when submarine or airplane attacks could be made out of the sun without being seen. Six fighter planes would be launched just before sunup to fly combat air patrol over the task force, and soon after, a number of dive-bombers and torpedo planes armed with aerial depth charges would be sent up to fly searches out a hundred miles or more looking for submarines or surface vessels. After the planes were off the deck and general quarters secured, the smoking lamp was lit, and breakfast was served. Coffee and beans, sometimes Spam, occasionally dried eggs, dry cereal with powdered milk, prunes or some other kind of dried or canned fruit. Oranges or apples if you had been in port recently.

Then the day's work began, cleaning and polishing, repairing the equipment for which you were responsible, belting ammunition, providing working parties for one job after another, shifting ammunition in the magazines, restowing the heavy towing cable, and the dreaded chipping detail. Peacetime navy ships were beautifully painted inside and out, and the lower decks were covered with a heavy red linoleum kept at a high shine. The Pearl Harbor attack, however, had taught the terrible lesson that paint and linoleum burn fiercely, giving off a heavy toxic smoke, and so after December 7 all ships were ordered to get rid of all the interior paint, except in the light green officers' quarters, and all the linoleum.

The interior of a carrier, like other warships, is a maze of hatches, welded supports, air ducts, cables, pipes, and tangled metal, all covered generously with several coats of white or gray paint, and to chip it all off, flake by flake, with a flat scraping tool—bent at a right angle and sharpened on one end—was a labor of the damned. It was hot inside the ship, and the men stripped to their skivvies, rags around their heads, and chipped away—clink, clink, clink, damn!—hour after hour. It was maddening work, as I found after I got off the flight deck crew, difficult, endless, seemingly pointless, and when it was finished after many months in which it took up every spare hour, the linoleum ripped off the rusty decks, the compartments with their raw steel plates and rusting, pitted, paint-flecked bulkheads were depressing, as if the ship had already been burned out.

Everyone stayed on deck as much as possible, watching the task force spread out over the ocean, which never ceased to be interesting, even after months of steaming. The carrier was in the center, and two or three cruisers—the Salt Lake City, Northampton, Chester, or Pensacola—were usually with us, plunging steadily along on both sides. The destroyers, ten or twelve, raced about on the flanks, ahead and to the stern, listening for submarines, transferring material and personnel, and serving as plane guards to pick up the crews of crashed planes.

We fueled at sea, and occasionally a big tanker, named after a faraway American river—the Platte or the Cimarron—would come alongside, some twenty-five to fifty feet away, and with both ships still under way, pitching and rolling toward each other, riggings sometimes fouled, these thousands of tons of mass would send rubber hoses across and pump fuel and aviation gas out of the tanker into the carrier. Sometimes, as we became more adept, a cruiser or destroyer would get fuel at the same time on the other side of the tanker, or would take fuel from the carrier herself on the side away from the tanker. The waves between the ships in this operation were huge, and standing on the flight deck of the carrier, you could watch the great bulk of the tanker rise up above you, and then crash down. It was blue-water seamanship at its best, always pleasant to watch how smartly it was done. It permitted our ships to stay at sea much longer and to operate while there without having to run at slow speeds to conserve fuel. It also meant that, keeping radio silence, you could disappear for months at a time in the distances of the ocean, to appear, suddenly, somewhere where you weren't expected or wanted.

This is what the *Enterprise* did at the beginning of February 1942, on the first major American carrier raid of the war, the attack on the Marshall Islands—Roi, Wotje, Kwajalein—where atomic bombs would be tested many years later. We had been down to Samoa escorting troop ships and looking longingly at the green tropical islands off in the far distance. The *Yorktown* had come around from the Atlantic, and after we joined with her, we moved to the north together. The run in to the islands began in the evening and continued at thirty-three knots all night long. Here for the first time I sweated through the night before the battle in one of the great carriers.

The crew's compartments were aft, where, lying in your bunk with the whole stern of the ship vibrating, jumping up and down, really, the propeller shafts turning at near maximum rpms, sleep was fitful. Restless with the noise and rattle, the quiet shush of the air ducts bringing fresh air to compartments where all portholes had long been welded shut, there was general uneasiness, communicated by endless nervous shifting in the bunks and constant movement back and forth to the head in the dim red glare of the night-lights. During battle conditions the red lights went out, and the blue battle lamps here and there created an eerie, never-to-be-forgotten, spooky feeling, sweat dripping down into your eyes from under your gray steel World War I helmet, the stale chemical smell of the fireproofed canvas covers of the bulky gray kapok-filled life jackets tied tightly up under your chin.

Reveille was a relief. A rush to get up to the deck, hoping to see the islands we were attacking, but there were only the familiar blue water and the escort vessels. The Marshalls were still many miles away, islands attacked but

The USS *Enterprise* ready to launch her planes in 1942. (*Naval Institute Collection*)

never seen. The strike force went off about 0500—a few torpedo planes carrying bombs for a high-level bombing attack, some dive-bombers with a yellow five-hundred-pound bomb under the fuselage, a handful of fighters to provide air cover—and the cruisers moved in to shell the landing fields on some of the islands. It seemed a mighty air armada to us then, who had not yet seen the sky filled from horizon to horizon with carrier planes at the end of the war on their way to the Japanese mainland. Now, for the attack, I was released from plane-pushing duties to help load bombs on the torpedo planes, hoisting them up and locking them into the bomb rack, inserting the fuses and threading the long copper arming wire through the holes in the fuse vanes, tightening up the sway brackets. Off in the distance the strike group was no bigger than a fist held up in the sky.

The *Enterprise* was still after her strike had been launched. Work stopped, and everyone waited nervously to see if we had been spotted by the enemy. Ship's radar was primitive in those days, but we did have it, and the Japanese did not—one of our few advantages—and this morning it kept telling us that the skies were clear, that the Japanese planes had been caught on the ground and their ships in the great anchorage inside the circular atoll. Then the wait began for the return of our own planes, and about mid-morning a few fighters arrived, then some dive-bombers, and at last the torpedo planes. All eyes tried to count to see how many planes from the air group had been lost. A few, it turned out; not more than three or four.

The *Enterprise* turned into the wind, picked up maximum speed, cleared the flight deck, and raised the arresting cables to catch the planes' tailhooks. The hydraulic crash barriers three-quarters of the way up the deck came up with a swoosh, and the carrier began to take her air group aboard. The planes roared by in loose formation on the starboard side, a few hundred feet up, and as they passed the ship, began to peel off, one by one, to their port, flying around the ship and coming in low and aft, following the wake, onto the deck. The landing signal officer stood at the rear on the port side, facing aft, with two yellow paddles, one in each hand, giving visual signals to the incoming plane. Up a little, a bit to port, less power, cut.

The plane hit the deck heavily, its hook grabbed one of the elevated tailhook wires and pulled it out until the plane came to a stop. Men raced out to release the arresting wire, the tailhook retracted, the crash barriers went down, the plane taxied forward at high speed, slammed on the brakes, and the barrier came up just as the next plane was landing. A tricky and a dangerous business, but everything depended on doing it fast and doing it well. In peacetime the navy was miserly about every piece of equipment, but in wartime a badly wrecked plane went over the side instantly to clear room for the following plane.

How effective the strike had been no one seemed to know, and if they did, no one bothered to tell the crew, who filled what later times would call an information gap with scuttlebutt about monstrous battleships sunk in the channel, hundreds of planes exploding from direct hits while taxiing out to take off, disgraced and distraught Japanese admirals committing hara-kiri on the control tower to apologize to the emperor. Quite satisfying stuff, which made the morning seem extremely worthwhile, though in fact the few planes with their light bomb loads had done little harm.

After another small follow-up strike was launched, we were told to rearm all the torpedo planes with torpedoes, which were considered, as the Japanese had demonstrated at Pearl Harbor, the right weapons with which to sink warships. I was moving one of the stubby 21-inch aerial torpedoes that weighed two thousand pounds on a hydraulic lift across the oily, slippery hangar deck. Suddenly the 5-inch antiaircraft guns on the after starboard sponson above began firing, and the deck heeled sharply up fifteen degrees on that side as the ship turned abruptly to port to evade an attack.

My first real experience of a shooting war! The steep angle of the deck caused the heavy torpedo to slide down toward the port side, carrying me and the other man I was working with, with it. We lowered the hydraulic skid to the deck, but the torpedo still slid on the oily steel until we at last got some lashings on it and secured it to the rings in the deck used for tying down planes. There we stood, two sailors with a lashed-down torpedo, in the middle of the vast empty hangar deck, which was shifting rapidly from one crazy angle to another. We wanted to get the hell out of there but couldn't leave the torpedo with its live warhead for fear it would break loose and smash into a bulkhead and explode. We stayed, even though by then the smaller guns (.50-caliber machine guns) along the catwalk were firing.

You could measure the progress of an attack by the number and caliber of guns firing. As long as the five-inchers were booming, the enemy was still high and far away, but when the small-caliber guns (first the four-barreled deliberate one-point-ones—bang, bang, bang, bang—and then the fifties) began rattling away, it was time to put your head down. When someone ran out on the deck and began firing a pistol, which frequently happened, the attack was really closing in.

Water splashed in one of the openings in the hangar deck from a near miss. In a few minutes it was all over, and the *Enterprise*, undamaged, was on her way back to Pearl Harbor.

One of our torpedo planes flying a search vector did not return one bright blue day. We waited for it and the three men aboard hour after hour until we knew that it had surely run out of gas in an ocean where there was no place to land except on the deck of the *Enterprise*. Search planes were sent out, and destroyers patrolled for miles in all directions, but no trace of the plane was found and the men were assumed lost. When they turned up in Pearl Harbor about two months later, looking a bit thin but fit, we were all astounded. They had spent thirty days on their small yellow rubber raft, all three of them, with no rations or water at all, having lost everything when they ditched with engine failure. Rainwater, seabirds, and fish kept them going until purely by accident, in all that vastness, they washed ashore on a small island, losing their raft getting across the coral reef, and then, exhausted, flung up on the beach by a wave.

The March 23, 1942 issue of *Time* magazine referred to the pilot, an enlisted chief named Harold Dixon, as "a man that Bligh would fancy," and encouraged by this kind of doubtful praise, he published a book (with help from a ghostwriter) later in 1942 about the journey, making, so we heard, a fortune from it. The book made its way out to the squadron where everyone hooted and traded foolish quotes from Dixon's ghostwriter's purple pen. The book reported him as saying to his crew when they lay exhausted, emaciated and totally dehydrated on the beach of the island, "If there are Japs on this island, they'll not see an American sailor crawl. We'll stand, and march, and make them shoot us down like men-o'-warsmen." The squadron wits amused us for weeks with aping the way that men-o'-warsmen, a term most of us had never heard, would march to the center of the island and be shot down.

Entering Pearl Harbor after the Marshall raid was the most moving moment of the war for me; far more than Nagasaki, which was hard to take in, or Tokyo Bay. We were in whites, lined up at quarters on the flight deck, and as we came down the channel, the sunken and burned battleships along Ford Island in plain sight, the crews of the anchored ships, at quarters themselves, their white uniforms showing up against their gray ships, cheered us, one after another, again and again. The frustration of defeat and helplessness after Pearl Harbor, while the Japanese overran the entire western Pacific and sank our ships wherever they found them, in the Philippines or in Indonesia, was enormous. The raid by the *Enterprise* on the Marshalls was the first successful action by an American ship; small, yes, but it was enough to give the fleet a lift.

Exultation was brief for me. I had already been a plane-handler, but that was a noble occupation compared to mess cooking: three months in the galleys, literally, peeling and slicing potatoes in enormous machines, washing huge pots and pans for days at a time, carrying out garbage pails filled to the brim with slops to be dumped over the side at night, serving food to the endless lines of sailors coming through to be fed and making nasty remarks about what you gave them.

Everyone did it, but mess cooking was real exile. You had to move to the mess halls with your bedding, stow your hammock in the nets there, and sleep in it at night, one of the few places in the modern navy where hammocks were used. The food-serving operation ran night and day, with watches coming on and going off duty every four hours, and only the exhaustion of eighteen-hour days of heavy labor made sleep possible in compartments where the lights were never out and people came and went constantly.

Good luck sent me after a month of work in the vegetable locker (peeling potatoes) to the galley of the chief petty officers' quarters, where the work was lighter, the nights uninterrupted, and a tip given by the chiefs every month for satisfactory service.

One of the most disagreeable jobs was handling the huge galvanized garbage cans filled with slop. It took two men to get them up the slippery narrow ship's ladders, step by painful step, with some inevitable spillage on you, and the deck, along the way to where they could be emptied over the side, to leeward, of course, not always an easy place to find in the dark if the ship was maneuvering and the wind was shifting. This was done at night to avoid leaving a trail of our presence in the ocean.

One night my fellow garbage handler and I fell on a steep ladder. In a failed attempt to keep the can from spilling, Whitey slipped and hit his mouth on the edge of the can, knocking out one of his upper-front teeth. The ship's dentist did only fillings and extractions, no cosmetic work, and so Whitey spent the next eight hours of the liberty we got every month or two when we came into Pearl going to a Honolulu dentist to get a false tooth installed. This was both a painful and an expensive way to spend what little liberty and money he had—even though we were by that time seamen first class making all of fifty-four dollars a month—and I used to argue with him long and earnestly, in the way that only a young man who knows nothing could, that it was pointless to waste his time and money in this fashion. Better to wait until the war was over and you knew whether you would survive to use a false tooth, ran my foolish and boring refrain.

But Whitey was not only stubborn, he was, it turned out to my vast surprise, hugely vain, and though small and nondescript physically, like the rest of us—we did not look at all like the sailors we saw dancing their lives away in the movies!—he could not bear the thought of being what he considered mutilated. I know now that he was right, but then so was I, without really knowing anything, for, having taken up the trade of a cook, he was killed along with Dallas, the head cook, by an armor-piercing bomb that exploded in the chiefs' galley the following October at the Battle of Santa Cruz.

A month at sea, cruising back and forth across the International Date Line, up and down over the equator, inducted with some strenuous naval horseplay into "The Ancient and Honorable Order of Shellbacks," a quick air attack on some little island, Wake or Marcus, and then back to Pearl for supplies and a brief liberty.

Honolulu in those days was more out of Somerset Maugham than Gauguin, but it seemed the proper setting for the heroes we felt we were, dressed in fresh white uniforms, rushing onto the buses and roaring down to Canal Street. A few minutes were spent in the New Congress Hotel, where the "French line" went up the long wooden stairs on the right, and the "old-fashioned line" ascended the left staircase. (Such sophistication! What could the Old Congress have been like?) Going once through each line— take your choice of the order—was considered a sign of true manhood, and the really virile went right back into the line rather than getting a few drinks before returning to the service of Venus.

On to the honky-tonks with the jukeboxes, the fights between sailors from different ships, and several bottles of the unspeakable local brew, Primo Beer, no hard liquor being sold. Dirty, bedraggled, and obscenely noisy we made our way back to the navy yard by late afternoon, ran the gauntlet of the marine guards at the gate who took out their frustrations with clubs on sailors looking for a fight, and then crowded into the fifty-foot motor launches that took us at last back to ships with names as epic—*Enterprise, Yorktown, Salt Lake City, Pensacola*—as those at Trafalgar or Jutland. Weighed soberly, Honolulu liberty was not much, but it had the effect of making us glad to be, as sailors always are, aboard ship again.

I fancied myself quite a dancer at the time, though the hornpipe had passed, and I found my way in time to the servicemen's club—the USO that had just been opened—to dance with the local Portuguese girls who volunteered to mingle with the sailors. Honolulu was an old liberty port, long familiar with naval antics ashore, and while nothing we did could any longer surprise the outrage-hardened citizenry, they wanted as little to do with us as possible. Most especially, they did not want us even to look at their daughters. Unaware of what it meant to be a sailor in Honolulu, I thought I cut quite a fine nautical figure and was crestfallen when I tried to make a date with one of the beautiful Portuguese girls, only to learn that her father would rather see her date one of the lepers from Molokai than a sailor. But my heart was not broken.

In April we put to sea and to our surprise went north for a change. Morale dropped conspicuously low with the news that Bataan had surrendered. As it became cold and colder, woolen gloves and winter uniforms long stowed away in seabags in storage lockers appeared. White water broke over the flight deck as the ship rose and fell in heavy green seas. One morning there was another carrier, the USS *Hornet* (CV 8), sister ship of the *Enterprise*, running alongside, about a hundred yards away. Instead of the usual pale blue-and-white naval aircraft, her deck was loaded with khaki-colored twin-engine army light bombers, B-25s, from a point forward of the island, in two rows, all the way to the stern. We assumed that they were intended for delivery somewhere in the Aleutians, but the public address system soon announced, there being no need for secrecy since there was no one we could tell and no way we could tell them, that this was an army squadron commanded by Col. James Doolittle, to be launched for an attack on Tokyo after we carried it to a point five hundred miles off the Japanese mainland. The *Enterprise* was to provide combat air patrols and antisubmarine patrols for the *Hornet* since she could launch none of her own planes stowed away on the hangar deck.

We were tremendously excited, not only at the idea of hitting Tokyo itself but also at the danger of going so close to Japan. But we were technicians, and it was the technical problem that really intrigued us. Could the heavy planes with a bomb load of two thousand pounds, even when stripped of guns and armor, get to Japan and then make it to the nearest safe landing point in China? Even before that, could such heavy planes designed for long landing strips get off a short carrier deck? The B-25s spotted farthest forward had a run of only about three hundred feet before dropping off the bow, which was about the minimum run needed for even the much smaller carrier planes designed for this work. Sailors, like stockbrokers, work everything out by betting, and there was soon heavy money down on both sides: would they make it, would they not? The odds were that the B-25s wouldn't have been on the *Hornet* if there had not been tests somewhere, but with all the skepticism of an old salt about anything the services did, I put down ten dollars at even money that less than half of them would get off.

April 18 was a cold and windy morning: near gale-force winds, gray and blue everywhere, with high dark green waves and the real taste and smell of the northern ocean. We were spotted some six hundred miles off the Japanese coast by fishing boats serving as pickets and patrol craft. The light cruiser *Nashville*, with fifteen 6-inch guns in five turrets, three forward and two aft, looked the picture of naval warfare in the age of steam as she came up to flank speed—about thirty-five knots—turned sharply to port, and began firing. Signal flags crackled as they ran up and down on the halyards, black smoke blew in the wind, yellow flashes came out of the gun barrels, and salvo after salvo missed the little boats bobbing on the waves, now in sight, now hidden. They were not easy targets. The rounds that hit were armor-piercing and went through the wooden hulls without exploding; and even though the cruiser fired more than a thousand six-inch projectiles, the little boats kept bobbing up and down. The *Enterprise's* fighters, the stubby little bee-like Grumman F4Fs, swarmed on the Japanese boats instantly and covered them with machine-gun fire.

Everyone assumed, however, that the *Nashville's* failure had given the Japanese time to radio warnings. After the war it became known that, screwed up themselves, they had not transmitted a warning, but the assumption on the American ships had to be that the Japanese now knew that two carriers were close to their shores and that we had better get out of there if we wanted to save the ships on which the Pacific war depended. The range was a hundred miles or so too long for the B-25s, but the decision was made to risk it and launch anyway. So, turning into the gale, over forty knots by now, which helped the launch, the *Hornet* began to send the bombers off. The first plane, Doolittle's, didn't even use up the deck available. So powerful was the wind added to the full speed of the ship—about seventy-five knots combined—that the B-25s needed only to get up about thirty knots' speed to float off the deck like some great kites, only slowly moving ahead of the ship, which seemed to remain almost stationary below them. One after another the entire squadron went off, and we all cheered loudly, choked down a few patriotic tears, and I thought my ten dollars well lost in a good cause, as if I had actually contributed the money to success in the war.

We turned back at once to get out of range of the Japanese aircraft, and though we were told that Doolittle had bombed Tokyo, we heard no details about how most but not all of the planes made it to China until years afterward, when the entire story of the minor damage, but heavy blow to Japanese pride, became public.

Within a few days it was warm again, and after another brief stop at Pearl we departed, still with the *Hornet*, for the southwest Pacific, where the battle to contain the Japanese drive to the south and the east—Australia, New Guinea, and the Solomon Islands—was shaping up. By now the surface ships in Indonesia, that is, the cruisers *Houston* and *Marblehead*, having been annihilated, and the *Prince of Wales* and *Repulse* having been sunk off Malaya, the war on both sides was being fought by task forces centered on aircraft carriers, which maneuvered to locate the enemy and get in the first strike, sinking or damaging his carriers. Two of our four active carriers in the Pacific, the *Lexington* and *Yorktown*, were already in the Coral Sea, off the eastern end of New Guinea, trying to block two Japanese fleets coming at them from opposing directions. We were being sent to equal the odds and to come in from the east to surprise the Japanese two-carrier task force coming south from Truk.

Wartime cruising had settled down to a routine in which boredom and tiredness ate away at life at sea. Stripped of paint and linoleum, rusting everywhere, constantly hot from cruising near the equator, with few air blowers open below deck, shuddering with high-speed maneuvers in a way that knocked over anything set on shelf or table, the ships and life aboard them began to get to us. Fresh food lasted only a few days after we had been in port; we had only salt water to wash and shave in, with the irritation of sandy saltwater soap; there was no entertainment of any kind, only work and sleep. Men began to get irritable.

Dungarees and blue work shirts, the standard uniform of the day, were never ironed, only washed and dried together in a great bag that had to be rummaged through to find those with your name stenciled on them. Put on clean and dry, they were soaking wet from the heat in a few minutes. White hats were dyed an anemic purple, and white socks were forbidden in order to avoid the flashes of white on the flight deck that would betray the presence of the ship to a snooper aircraft. Heat rash tormented everyone, particularly around the waist where several layers of wet clothing twisted and pulled inside the belt. A story circulated that when the heat rash—a quarter of an inch high and several inches wide, red and angry—girdled your waist, you died. No one believed it, but everyone kept a careful eye on the progress of the rash around his middle.

No one died, but every free moment was spent somewhere where the cooling breeze could blow over the rash and the sun could dry it out. Lacking any movies and music to entertain us, we gambled. It became the only relief from the tedium of what now was becoming not weeks but months at sea without even seeing land in the distance. I was a more enthusiastic than skillful poker player, but I loved the game, as I did bridge, and even though I regularly lost my money in games in one small compartment or another about the ship, the first glimpse of the five cards in draw poker or the hole card in stud poker were the high moments, ironically, of days that were routinely filled with the real adventure of accidents and frequent death.

Death lived on an aircraft carrier operating in wartime conditions. One day a plane would crash taking off, and the lucky pilot lost no more than an eye on his telescopic sight mounted in front of him. The next day a plane landing on deck would drop a wheel strut into the catwalk and run screeching up it for a hundred feet. A mangled crewman would be carried away. A thoughtless step backward on the flight and hangar decks where the planes were turning up led to decapitation and gory dismemberment by propeller. Planes went out on patrol and were never heard of again. Death took many forms, but I think I first really came to know him on a day when I was standing on the flight deck and a Dauntless dive-bomber flew across the ship to drop a message about something seen on a patrol.

Once ships had put to sea, strict radio silence was maintained except for certain high-frequency VHF short-range transmissions used to direct the CAP (Combat Air Patrol) of fighters, close by the ship. Beanbags trailing long red streamers were used for message drops in order to preserve radio silence. As the dive-bomber came across the ship at about 120 knots, with the starboard wing sharply down to give the radioman an open field to throw the message bag on the flight deck, the down wing caught, ever so slightly, just a tick, the railing on the catwalk at the very edge of the ship. Just a flicker, but it was enough. In an instant the plane was in the water off the starboard side, broken in half between the radioman and the pilot, neither of whom, knocked out by the crash, heads hanging limply forward, moved. Then in an instant both pieces were gone, the water was unruffled, and the ship sailed on. The quickness with which active life, so much energy and skill in the banking plane, disappeared as if it had never been stunned me.

It was the instantaneous contrast of something and nothing that caught my attention, and like some eighteen-year-old ancient mariner, I went around for days trying to tell people what had *really* happened, how astounding it was. The response was polite; death was a grave matter to everyone and never lightly dismissed. But no one, quite rightly, wanted to philosophize or make too much of what was common and likely to be the end of all of us, much sooner than later.

FIVE

Midway

The tightly controlled fear of death was stirred up with the news a few days later that the *Lexington*, commissioned in the early 1920s, had been sunk by aircraft and the *Yorktown* damaged in the Battle of the Coral Sea, the first of the great carrier battles of the Pacific war. The *Lexington* was a much loved ship in the navy—as her sister ship the *Saratoga* was not, for unknown reasons—a "good ship" it was said, and the news of her sinking was felt as a personal blow, particularly to the many aboard the *Enterprise* (a relatively new ship, commissioned in 1938), who had served on the "Lady Lex." Felt too because she was the first American carrier to go down, making clear our own vulnerability, increasing the odds to at least six Japanese carriers against only three American.

Again, however, our desire for simple revenge was thwarted when the *Enterprise* and *Hornet* turned and began making a high speed run back to Pearl Harbor. It seemed to us once more like craven cowardice, and there was a good deal of muttering. But as we approached Pearl, where there was, we were told, to be no liberty this time, the rumor mill began to whisper a fantastic story. The Japanese fleet, it was said, was about to attack Midway Island, with a diversionary move on the Aleutians, and we, having broken their code, were going to lie off Midway and surprise them. Intelligence officers contend that there could have been no leaks at this time, but I remember exactly the occasion on which I was told, with full details about ships and dates. Modern historians of the war still assume that secrecy on this critical matter was carefully maintained, that our success at Midway resulted from it, but I can testify that the deepest navy secret—that we had broken the Japanese code and were reading their messages—was widely known among the enlisted men, and the proposed strategy and tactics for the coming battle learnedly and gravely discussed by the admirals of the lower deck, who were, on the whole, as always, of the opinion that the officers' plan would not work!

A few days out of Pearl a destroyer came alongside with the mail that was our lifeline back to familiarity. My best letters came from my mother, who was a good correspondent, typing long and interesting letters about the dogs, cats, cattle, and horses on the ranch, the neighbors, and plans for the spring and the ranch's new buildings. A few hours later the letters worked their way down to the divisional compartments and were passed out by the mail orderly—"Smith, she's run off with a marine"—and now, these fifty years later, the feelings are still so hot under the ashes that I can write only with the greatest difficulty of the first letter I opened, from my stepfather (he did not often write), dated April 28, 1942. The words hit me like a hammer:

> I am writing this in Saratoga on Sunday morning following the funeral of our Dear. . . . Then I went over to get in the wood and do the chores. The door was locked. My first thought was it was a joke. I called to her and no answer. Then I tapped the door with my overshoe and asked to be let in. No answer. Then I got alarmed and kicked the door in. Mother was laying in the dining room Dead. I ran to her and felt her pulse. She was cold as marble. I felt her head and it was likewise. She had shot herself in the temple with the 22 pistol you gave her. I did not touch the gun. The whole sight was one awful shock and I will not describe the scene further in this letter. I hunted for a note for a few minutes and then lit out for town. I ran until I was ready to keel and then got control of myself to go into a walk.

The old letter still has the burns where I crumpled it and put it in a bulk-head ashtray before I was finished reading it, only to return to dig it, smoldering, out and go through each of the awful details. A letter I opened later from my mother, written a few days before her suicide on April 22, gave no indications of anything particularly wrong, and apparently she had bottled whatever it was up in herself, in the way that in all the old photos of groups she is hard to spot, lurking, I realized long afterwards, in the background, away in the corner. It was, of course, despair, despair with all the many things that had gone wrong in life and could never be put right, but I didn't know that at the time and hunted for particular reasons, including blaming myself for having left her. The telegram telling me of her death arrived in the mail months later.

Feelings of heavy emotional pressure were intensified by being on a ship in the middle of an ocean, on the way to a great battle, trying to deal with a

Kate Fletcher Peters Kernan (1900–1942), my mother, with neighbors Vernon Swanson and Louis Clough, center (killed in France in 1944), and an unfortunate local bear.

mysterious event, the body already buried a month earlier. Having to do something, I blundered down into the pale green officers' quarters, where enlisted men were prohibited without a pass, and found my way to the Catholic chaplain's rooms. I was not devoutly religious, but I had been raised a Catholic in order to please my stepfather, and now seemed the time, if ever, to call on religion for help not to be found elsewhere. The chaplain was napping. Startled to see a crying distraught young sailor, he asked first if I had a pass, which I did not. Being young, I expected help, and insisted that he provide it in some tangible form like getting me leave to go home, which he could not, of course, arrange.

The old chief of the ordnance gang, Murphy, sipping moosemilk, was more sympathetic and more practical. He took me off mess cooking—sending some other poor devil down to the galleys—and gave me a day off, which I spent sitting on a sponson and staring at the ocean rolling by. I slept well, which made me feel guilty that I lacked feeling.

A second day off was not thought good for me by the assembled wisdom of the ordnance gang sitting in solemn conclave wearing the red-cloth helmets that were the symbol of our trade. So I was put to work again along with everyone else, getting .50-caliber ammunition up from the magazines, taking it out of its wooden boxes, opening the greased tin inner containers and paper cartons, and then using hand and automatic belters to shove the bullets into the connecting metal links for the machine guns of the fighter planes in the coming battle. Black tips were armor piercing; blue, incendiary; red, tracer; and plain, ball. We made up different combinations for different purposes, using more tracer where it was important to be able to see from the burning tip of the bullet where the fire stream was going, more armor piercing and incendiary for the hits, and ball to keep the barrels of the guns from burning out too quickly with all this hard, hot stuff.

Working away, eating, sleeping, and in a short time talking and joking with the rest of the ordnance gang, my mother's death drifted away from me. We are much simpler mechanisms than we think, preserving life and seeking what meaning we can find in it. The dead must bury the dead because no one else pauses long enough to do so. Guilt is inevitable, but the real danger, I quickly found, was in feeling that you cannot move on away from what you cannot endure, letting deep emotions get too tangled and blocked.

On May 26 we were back in Pearl. Halsey, who had been standing for weeks on the bridge in his skivvy shorts trying to cool the allergic rash that was covering his body—he must have been more nervous than he appeared to be—went ashore to the hospital. He had become a hero to the crew by then, for no apparently good reason except that he was familiar, and so his departure seemed ominous. Nimitz came aboard, and we all stood to quarters to watch medals being presented to various worthies. Later, Spruance appeared as the new admiral commanding Task Force 16, built around the *Enterprise* and *Hornet*, for the Battle of Midway.

Someone saw fit to give me a two-hour compassionate liberty after we reached Pearl, time enough to race into Honolulu in a taxi to the Mackay office (naval communications were never used for personal matters of enlisted men) to cable some borrowed money home to help with funeral expenses and let my stepfather know that his messages had been received, that grief had spread as far as it was likely to for this death. The brass would never have let me off the ship if they thought I or anyone else had the slightest knowledge about the Japanese plans and the coming battle. How astounded they would have been that everyone in the crew knew about the code and the plans! Even so, all precautions were taken to seal off the ship lest something somehow leak out, and though it was little enough, I was always grateful to whomever it was who made the tremendous argument that must have been necessary to get me ashore in those tense circumstances.

The time in port was short and filled with all-hands details provisioning the ship, refilling the magazines, getting stores and fuel aboard. The bright floodlights burned all night as one lighter after another came alongside, while the workmen from the yard installed new guns and equipment. But no one complained, for once, and excitement shone in the men's eyes. By the late morning of May 28, lighters still alongside, we were under way, steaming out of that deep and narrow channel that leads south out of the great harbor at Pearl to the open Pacific Ocean. Though we were unaware of it, at the same time (May 29 Japanese time), Isoroku Yamamoto on his flagship, *Yamato*, the largest ship in the world—seventy thousand tons, nine 18.1-inch guns—was leading the Japanese fleet out of Yashiro-jima through the Bungo Channel on the way to Midway, twenty-five hundred miles to the east. The *Yorktown* was being patched up in the dry dock at Pearl and would follow in a few days, with yard workmen still aboard making repairs, to complete the American fleet.

Once under way, we continued belting machine-gun ammunition obsessively, like some rite of war, piling up huge mounds of ammunition ready for use in the planes. We also piled up an enormous amount of trash that had to be burned, long tow targets filled with pasteboard cartridge cartons pulled like Chinese festival dragons laboriously down the passageways and ladders to the ship's incinerator to be burned at night when the smoke would not give away the position of the ship to submarines or scout planes. Big jobs always produce new shit details, and the eyes of authority—perhaps because they had overlooked the rules and felt pity for me a few days earlier—found me out instantly and dispatched me to work shoveling tons of paper into the incinerator all night long.

The trash contained bullets here and there, missed in the sorting, and after these lay in the hot fire for a time, they exploded. Since they had no firm backing when they exploded, the bullets lacked the force to go through the insulated steel sides of the furnace, but if by chance one came through the door of the incinerator when it was open, it would maim anyone it hit. The job required two sailors, dressed only in skivvies in the boiling heat that was filled with the stale smell of trash, flames lighting the small space weirdly. One man opened the door of the furnace and then slammed it closed, instantly, once a shovelful of trash had gone in. The other sailor, me, threw a shovel load in the furnace and then quickly dropped to the deck to avoid any rounds that might have cooked off since the last shovelful was thrown in. The pops were loud and frequent, and eight hours of shovel-drop-pop from sunset to sunrise jangled the nerves. But the danger was less, much less, than the frustration of being occupied with trash disposal while going into what we all knew would be one of the great naval battles of all time.

After burning paper all night, I got a few hours of sleep on the morning of June 4 before going up to the ordnance shack to help arm the planes. This was the big day when the tactics of U.S. naval air that had been developed over twenty years were at last put into practice and failed. Knowing that the Japanese fleet intended to attack and take Midway to prevent Doolittle-type raids and draw out our fleet for the big surface battle they always sought, the three American carriers—*Enterprise*, *Hornet*, and the battered *Yorktown*, all sister ships and the only three American carriers left in the central Pacific—had steamed more than a thousand miles and taken up station to the north and east of Midway at the aptly named Point Luck. Though we were apprehensive, the hubristic Japanese were completely unaware of our presence because, having beaten us so easily for so long, they were careless, and because of poor scouting. Their position was established just after dawn by land-based planes flying out of Midway. The carriers turned into the wind and, once the CAP was in the air, the *Enterprise* and *Hornet* began just about 0700 to launch a model carrier-based air strike.

The torpedo planes from my squadron (VT-6), being slowest, went first: fourteen TBDs loaded with torpedoes to sink ships. Each carried two men, the pilot and the radioman-gunner. The mid-seat observer-bombardiers were left behind that day, presumably to save weight but in truth to save lives, for everyone half knew what was coming. The Douglas "Devastators"—how ironic the name—were obsolete, slow, only about a hundred knots, and not highly maneuverable, in contrast to the Japanese fighter planes, the remarkable Zeros, that would be among them before they came into range of the antiaircraft guns of the Japanese fleet.

Everyone knew that a new, much improved torpedo plane, the Grumman

Pilots of Torpedo Squadron Six on the deck of the *Enterprise* just before the Battle of Midway. *Left to right, second row, are:* Ensign Holder, Ensign Brock, Lieutenant (junior grade) Heck, Lieutenant Reiley, Lieutenant Commander Lindsey (commanding), Lieutenant Ely, Lieutenant (junior grade) Rombach, Ensign Macpherson, and Chief Aviation Pilot Schaefer. *Left to right, front row, are:* Ensign Prickett, Machinist Mueller, Machinist Winchell, Ensign Morris, Lieutenant (junior grade) Thomas, Ensign Hodges, Lieutenant (junior grade) Eversole, Chief Machinist Smith, and Lieutenant Laub.

TBF, the "Avenger," was ready for the fleet. One section of the *Hornet* torpedo squadron (VT-8) had already gotten the new planes and had flown out to Midway, from where they too attacked the Japanese fleet on June 3, though with no better success than the carrier squadrons.

All the ground crew, aware that this was the big day, were out to see the pilots and crews off, and as he walked by, Winchell, one of the squadron's several enlisted pilots recently made warrant officers, borrowed my cigarette lighter for luck. The commander of the squadron, Lt. Comdr. E. E. Lindsey, was taped from his waist to his neck after a crash a few days earlier. Bad eyesight had caused him to try to land at an odd angle to the flight deck, but he would not give up the attack he had trained for, for so many years.

After the torpedo planes cleared the deck, the dive-bombers of Bombing and Scouting Six, thirty-three in all, went off, the scouts with two one-hundred-pound bright yellow bombs under the wings and a five-hundred-pounder under the fuselage, the bombers with a single yellow one-thousand-pounder. Then the obsolescent little fighters, ten F4Fs, no match for the Zeros, clattered off. The tactics worked out over the years called for a concerted attack. The torpedo planes were to circle and then attack the Japanese fleet from all directions at sea level, not more than a hundred feet off the water. The dive-bombers were to come out of the sun at twenty thousand feet when attention was focused on the attacking torpedo planes, while the fighters were to fly air cover, engaging the Japanese fighters and preventing them from getting into the dive-bombers and the torpedo planes, lumbering and slow, flying straight and level during the time they were releasing their fish.

Timing and communication were everything, and despite years of practice, both were bad from the start. The different squadrons got separated at once. As we watched, the torpedo planes, being the slowest, formed up and took off alone to find the Japanese fleet, which they did by an error of navigation. Being low on gas by the time they got to the Japanese carriers some time just after 0900, they started their attack at once without knowing where the dive-bombers or the fighters were. The Japanese Combat Air Patrol of Zeros came down on them as they began their runs. None of our planes made a hit, or if they did the torpedoes did not explode.

We waited for them on the deck of the *Enterprise*, with an eye toward the *Hornet* nearby, and the *Yorktown* several miles away to the west, which launched her air group later to provide another strike. Our fighters came back first, intact, which seemed odd, and then one, two, three, and finally four torpedo planes straggled in separately, and that was it. The last of the planes was so badly shot up that it was deep-sixed immediately after it landed. One pilot, Winchell, was later picked up out of the water, sixty pounds lighter following seventeen days adrift in a raft after he was shot down. So, the total losses were nine out of fourteen crews.

The size of the loss was unimaginable, and even when the crews in a condition of shock told us what kind of a slaughter it had been, it was unbelievable. It became real when one of the surviving torpedo pilots, a bushy-mustached warrant officer, came out of his cockpit with his .45 automatic out and charged up the ladder to the bridge shouting that he was going to kill the lieutenant who had commanded the fighter escort. He was prevented by force from doing it, but the whole mess was out in an instant; that the torpedo planes had attacked alone; that the fighters had remained at a high altitude where there were no Japanese fighters, they had all gone down to shoot up the TBDs at sea level; and that while VT-6 was dying, the fighters decided there was no opposition that day and turned around and flew back to the *Enterprise*. The whole matter has remained, I understand, an issue in naval aviation to this day, but on the *Enterprise* on the morning of June 4, 1942, there was no doubt that the fighters had failed badly, and the torpedo planes had paid the price.

Around noon came the clanging alarm, the bugle call, "All hands man your battle stations," and then a few minutes later, "Bandits at twenty miles and closing, stand by to repel enemy air attack." But we were not the target that day. The *Yorktown*, about ten miles to port, was between us and the Japanese fleet, and she took the full weight of the attack. How glad we secretly were that it was not us. We stood on the deck and watched as in a movie the flashes and smoke from the antiaircraft guns in the distance. The *Yorktown* heeled over in sharp turns, taking evasive action, while near misses exploded around her, and attacking planes blew up in bright flares. Not all the bombs missed, and when it was over in less than half an hour, the *Yorktown* was down on the port side, dead in the water, and there were holes in her flight deck large enough to make it impossible for her to land her own planes. She was patched up at once and by 1400 was moving under her own power again, only to be hit by two torpedoes launched by the second and last Japanese strike. Even then she didn't go down until a submarine finished her off on the morning of the seventh.

Within a few minutes after the first attack on the *Yorktown*, her dive-bombers and ours began arriving in small clusters and singly. Shot up, some landing in the water, out of gas, some crashing on deck with failing landing gear or no tailhooks and being pushed over the side instantly to make room for the others coming in. But now the mood was triumphant. The bomber pilots could hardly contain themselves. They were shouting and laughing as they jumped out of the cockpit, and the ship that had been so somber a moment before when the torpedo planes returned became now hysterically excited.

The dive-bombers had found the Japanese carriers, and they had sunk three of them, getting to them in classic style, out of the sun while they were trying to launch their own planes and when they were occupied with the torpedo planes and other attacking land-based planes coming out of Midway. It was over in an instant. Each of the three Japanese carriers—caught with bombs and torpedoes on the deck instead of being stored away in the magazines, with gasoline in the lines that ought to have been drained and flooded with CO_2—went up like tinder. And in the afternoon the bombers went back and finished off the fourth and last carrier. Four of the six carriers that had carried out the attack on Pearl Harbor—the *Kaga* and *Akagi*, *Hiryu* and *Soryu*—were all burning and would sink before the next morning.

We were exultant, not just at the revenge for Pearl Harbor, sweet as that was, but at our renewed sense of power and superiority over the Japanese fleet. No one doubted by now that it would be a long war, but to everyone on the ships at Midway it was clear that we would win.

But a lot of old ideas were swept away on June 4. For one, our torpedo planes, the old TBDs, were death traps, slow, underarmed, and lacking in maneuverability. The Zeros had shot them down at will, not only the *Enterprise* squadron but also the squadrons from the *Yorktown* and *Hornet* as well. VT-8, the *Hornet* squadron, became famous for losing all of its fifteen planes and men except Ensign Gay, who flew over the carrier he was attacking and crashed on the other side but managed to get out and hide under a cushion in his life jacket all day long, watching the Japanese ships go down. VT-3, off the *Yorktown*, also lost all of its thirteen planes and most of its crews.

In addition to the forty-two torpedo planes from the three carriers, the six-plane section of VT-8 flying the new TBFs out of Midway lost five of its planes and all but two of its men, while six army bombers, B-26s, modified to carry torpedoes, lost four planes and got no hits. Of the fifty-four torpedo planes that attacked the Japanese carriers on June 4, only seven returned to base, a loss rate of 87 percent, and none did any damage to their targets. If any got a hit, they had no effect, for the torpedoes were themselves deficient and either broke up or failed to explode.

The failure of our torpedoes on planes and submarines during the first three years of the war—which everyone in the fleet knew and talked about—and the refusal of the navy to acknowledge the problem and fix it, remain one of the scandals of the U.S. Navy. All that reckless heroism, with no chance of success even if things had gone well, instead of going about as badly as they could. The Japanese torpedo, the "long lance," worked, and the Japanese pilots put them home, but from that day at Midway on, our navy used airborne torpedoes rarely.

The fighters were little better. The little Grumman F4Fs were no match for the Zeros at Midway. It was the dive-bombers that emerged there as the primary weapon of naval aviation, and until the end of the war, dive-bombing with one type of plane or another remained the most effective weapon. Thirty some dive-bombers in the *Enterprise* group and the same number of the *York-*

town group—the *Hornet* bombers never found the target—were enough to do what was needed. Even their success, however, turned not on planning so much as on luck and a piece of rare good judgment by Lt. Comdr. Wade McClusky, the commander of Air Group 6. On course 240°, having gone to the point of no return, he decided to go on for another ten minutes, during which time he saw the wake of a Japanese destroyer eighteen-thousand feet below going northeast. He chose to follow it, and over the horizon saw that mighty Japanese fleet below him, taking on aircraft, unable to launch, its fighter protection all down at sea level tormenting the torpedo planes. Bombing and Scouting Five from the *Yorktown* arrived just a little later, and between them the bombers of Air Groups 5 and 6 did the work. I have always thought that if there were one single crucial act in the Pacific war it was Wade McClusky's turn northeast, and though I never heard of him again, I have often wished him a long and prosperous life.

Battles are always well planned, but their outcomes always turn on chance. Many years after the war, the Japanese reports on what happened at Midway appeared and made it clear that we had been a lot luckier there than we had known at the time. Hubris, that fatal overconfidence engendered by easy victories in the early months of the war, made the Japanese eager to draw out and destroy the remnants of the American fleet, which, they believed, would have only one carrier. So they did not worry when one of their scouts from a cruiser was accidentally late in being launched on the fatal morning of June 4. But it just happened to be the scout assigned to the sector that would have discovered our fleet.

After launching their first strike against Midway, still unaware of our presence and thinking that they had all the time in the world, they made a fatal decision to rearm with bombs the second strike that remained aboard for another attack on Midway, rather than arming them with torpedoes and holding them in readiness to strike any American carriers that might appear. To add to their blunders, they brought the first strike, low on gas, back aboard before launching the second. At that point they finally learned that we were out there and began frantically arming and fueling for a strike against our carriers. But it was too late. Our torpedo planes were already attacking them, and though they made no hits, they drew all the Zeros down to sea level from where they were flying CAP at high altitude. When our bombers arrived, there were no fighters to oppose them, and the carrier decks were crowded with planes, gas, bombs, torpedoes, and ammunition just waiting to explode.

The Japanese were brave men, but it is hard not to exult across fifty years at reading about the shouts of their lookouts, "Hell Divers!" and their panic as the crews looked up into the sun and saw the dive-bombers there, with the yellow bombs already in the air beneath the planes and on their way into the big red rising suns painted on their yellow flight decks. Hard too not to admire the way their great pilot and air planner, Comdr. Minoru Genda, met the disaster with the brief word *Shimatta*, "We goofed."

At the end of the first day of battle the *Enterprise* pilots and those from the *Yorktown* who had landed on the *Enterprise* after sinking the Japanese carriers stood in a long line, waiting to be debriefed, just outside the incinerator where I was back to lighting up for the night's inferno and preparing to duck the dull bullets that hadn't made it to the battle. These were heroes dressed in their khaki flight suits, carrying pistols and knives over their yellow Mae Wests, and describing with quick hands and excited voices how they had gone into their dives, released their bombs, and seen the Japanese flight decks open up in flames just below them. The slaves who carried the equipment of the Greek warriors at Salamis, or the rowers chained to their benches at Lepanto—those other epic naval battles where the West turned Asia back— could not have felt more envious or less heroic than I.

The Battle of Midway was fought and won in a few hours on the morning of June 4, and it was finished by sunset when the last of the Japanese carriers, the *Hiryu*, was gutted. But what is clear in hindsight was not certain to either fleet at that time. Before withdrawing, the Japanese tried to force a surface action, and we grappled for their remaining ships like a blind wrestler. An information officer on the *Enterprise* drew a map with chalk on the side of the island, so that all on deck could follow the battle, and we were fascinated; but every fifteen minutes the yeoman on the scaffold suspended from the top of the stack changed the location and size of the fleets.

As the information constantly changed and the range to the enemy increased or decreased, so did the armaments. Bomb size went from one-thousand-pounders to five-hundreds and back again on the dive-bombers within the space of an hour. This meant endless work for ordnancemen, which got me at last out of the incinerator. I happily ran back and forth trundling bombs and carrying belted ammunition for the machine guns, a part of the ordnance gang again, hopefully, since I had just been made a petty officer, third class (sixty dollars a month), never to return to the drudgery of general ship's duties again. Nothing in the next two days of the battle could match the first, though the excitement remained high and the level of activity feverish.

The Japanese fleet proved elusive. We caught only a couple of cruisers and destroyers and hammered them viciously.

The *Enterprise* returned to Pearl Harbor on the morning of June 13, my nineteenth birthday, but I already knew how quickly memories, even of the greatest things, fade and lose their reality. Aware during the battle that this was probably the greatest event I would ever be present at, I looked for some image to fix Midway in my mind, forever. As I did so, I was waiting for a bomb to come up the forward bomb elevator shaft, about three feet by four. I looked down the narrow shaft going several hundred feet from the bright sunlight of the day on deck to the depths of the ship, where, close to the keel, the bomb magazines were located. At the very bottom, a bright yellow bomb had just been put on the elevator, so that I seemed to be looking down an immensely long tunnel at a bright yellow spot, both beautiful and deadly at once, at the end. To this very moment I can see it as clearly as if I were still there, and for me that image is the famous Battle of Midway.

SIX

Sunk

After Midway we were a squadron without pilots or planes. When we returned to Pearl Harbor, the enlisted men of Torpedo Six were sent to the Naval Air Station at Kaneohe, on the windward side of Oahu, where waiting for us were a new set of pilots with a new type of plane. The few surviving pilots from the old squadron had gone back to the States, and except for a few old hands, the new ones were fresh from flight training and eager to get into the war.

The new plane was the Grumman TBF, aptly called the Avenger, considering what had happened to the torpedo planes at Midway. It looked like the latest thing in technology to us. Heavy bodied, square folding wings, it still carried three men, but the radio gunner was now down in a little compartment at the rear of the plane. Above him and slightly forward was the gunner's power turret containing a single .50-caliber machine gun. The pilot had two fifties in the wings. There was another seat forward of the turret and just behind the pilot designed for an observer. It was, in fact, immediately filled up with new radio gear for which there was no room elsewhere. The engine was much more powerful than the one in the old TBDs, and the plane could turn up 180 knots with a torpedo or full bomb load, carried in a long bomb bay in the belly with folding hydraulic doors. Every one of these features was to become grimly personal and real for me at one time or another, but for the moment they seemed only wonders of American engineering and production, light blue and white outside, green in, ingenious ways of overwhelming the Japanese.

The ground crews studied the manuals that came with every new plane, working long days getting used to its ways. We rode in them frequently to see how all the gear worked, from the smoke-laying equipment, which the navy still thought of as one of its tactical weapons, to the reel that paid out the lines to the tow targets used for aircraft and ship's gunnery practice. Both of these pieces of equipment were standard and were hated by those of us who installed and worked them. The smoke was toxic and acid enough to burn a pair of dungarees right off your ass, taking the ass with them if you weren't careful. The tow reel, its gears driven by a fiendish little propeller mounted outside the fuselage, let kinks develop in the tow wire that could, if you were careless, take a hand off when they were released.

Still, it was a wonderful free time. Kaneohe, just across the island and over the high cliffs—Nuuanu Pali—from Pearl, was all soft breezes, big surf, white beaches, bright sun every day. The barracks were concrete, spacious, clean, and cool. Discipline was incredibly lax, and gambling went on all night in the heads where the lights burned without interruption. For once I made a few dollars and even managed to get an overnight liberty in Honolulu. I soon learned why I had no trouble getting a pass. A curfew cleared the streets at 2000; the restaurants had no food and the bars no whiskey. I had a good time, however, renting a room in the posh though empty Alexander Young hotel, downtown, lying in a marble bath smoking a cigar and reading the *Police Gazette*, as naughty a magazine as I could find, but not very naughty.

Promotion was easy too in an expanding navy. Ratings were now given away with a stroke of a yeoman's typewriter, to the disgust of the old-timers who had often waited years for promotion. There was an argument in the ordnance shack one day about who would go down to the beach and fill some of the practice bombs with sand. No one wanted to go, heavy jobs with shovels and dirt being scrupulously avoided in the navy—if you liked that sort of thing there was always the army—and so Murph said that he would make me a petty officer, second class, if I would do it without bellyaching. I thought he was joking, but I did it anyway, and the next week the squadron orders listed my name and the new rating of aviation ordnanceman, second class, paying the munificent sum of seventy-four dollars a month.

At Kaneohe I drifted into a part-time flying arrangement. All regular flight personnel drew an additional half salary, known as "skins," as flight pay. The squadron had a few extra sets of skins beyond those needed for the regular pilots and flight crews, and these were passed around among the leading chiefs and various personnel from time to time. Even little fish like me had a chance to get half or quarter skins once in a rare while. But you had to put in at least four certified hours a month in the air to qualify. The flight logs were sacred books not to be tampered with, and so actual flight time could not be avoided. Sometimes planes were crammed with ten or twelve persons flying around the island for four hours to get their flight time in.

The new planes had a turret with a .50-caliber machine gun, but there were as yet no specially qualified aerial gunners. It was assumed, however, that any ordnanceman could at least operate the turret and the gun, even if he couldn't hit a barn door. So from time to time, needing to put in a few hours in the air, I began to be a gunner, complete with a leather flight jacket with my name and squadron stamped in gold on a patch on the breast, helmet and earphones, and a khaki flight suit. Most of the other ordnancemen remembered the lesson of Midway, and I had little competition for a job of which I was exceedingly proud. Most of the time, though, I worked away on the ground: clean guns, bore-sight the fixed guns, load bombs and torpedoes, unload bombs and torpedoes.

The idyll was over in a month or so, and in late July we packed up and went back to Pearl to go aboard, not the *Enterprise*, which had already sailed for the South Pacific, but the *Hornet*. The old system of keeping air groups and ships together—Air Group 6 went with CV 6, the *Enterprise*, and Air Group 5 went with CV 5, the *Yorktown*—around which fierce loyalties were built, was no longer possible, and the carriers now took whatever squadrons were trained and ready when they sailed. The Airedales became vagabonds from this time on. Squadrons were never again at home on a particular ship, or even in an air group.

Torpedo Squadron Six was for the moment a part of Air Group 8, which was made up of squadrons from a variety of ships. We did not like the *Hornet*, especially since the paint had never been chipped off her bulkheads. She was new and had come into the Pacific for the Doolittle Raid, and we now had to turn to on a second ship and spend weeks in the sweaty heat with chipping hammer and wire brush. The *Hornet*'s crew did not like us at first, either, but it soon ceased to matter, and since the *Enterprise* and *Hornet* were sister ships we could even have the same bunks in the same compartments we had had on the *Enterprise*. Still, it was different and therefore unsettling.

There still remained, it turned out, one shit detail I had not been on—no hard feelings, everybody went the full rounds—and now each time a plane landed or took off, I stood at the edge of the flight deck, just aft of the island, dressed in a huge cumbersome floppy white asbestos suit, complete with boots and a heavy helmet, with a glass visor to see through. You carried the helmet since it had no air supply and you would suffocate in it in a few minutes. In my other hand I had a long chain with a hook at the end. If a plane crashed and either caught fire or was in danger of catching fire, I put on the helmet, rushed under the plane, and secured the chain around the bomb. At the same time another man, also dressed in an asbestos suit, climbed up the wing of the plane to the cockpit and released the bomb. It then, in theory, fell to the deck, did not explode, and was pulled by my chain, which a number of volunteers had presumably taken hold of, out of the fire and the danger of explosion.

The whole drill had a desperate sound to it, and the asbestos suit had a number of seams and openings that would surely, I thought, let the fire get to me. Repeated, increasingly insistent questions from me about this matter got no answers from anyone in charge, and I stood at the after end of the island, by the mobile crane for clearing wrecks, for week after week of landings, looking and feeling like a circus clown, hat under arm, getting ready to perform. Fortunately, during the time I was on this detail planes crashed and I rushed in and hooked the chain on the bomb, but there was no fire. Never in my time in the service did I see anyone test one of these Daniel suits in a fiery furnace, and I think it just as well.

The ship was hot, but the nights were clear and cool, with a warm light breeze blowing on the flight deck. The stars were brilliant and the sky crowded with them. The southern heavens were now visible, and the different constellations made it seem as if we had steamed into some world other than that presided over by the North Star and the Big Dipper. To lie on the flight deck at night after a day at work in the heat, cooled by the wind and delighted by the tremendous streams of phosphorescence at the bows and sterns of the escort destroyers and cruisers, was more than pleasure. Mostly people on deck at night were silent, but now and then a remarkably free conversation about the meaning of war and life would start with someone you didn't know at all. The dark and anonymity were better than daylight for these matters. More open, more honest.

One day I noticed an unusually earnest member of the squadron, Nelson, lying in his bunk reading *How to Win Friends and Influence People*, a self-improvement book by Dale Carnegie, famous at the time. The smug idiocy of the title ensures the book the immortality of true kitsch. I knew it well and saw it again with that sinking feeling that comes from the simultaneous recognition of human need and the futility of trying to satisfy it. My mother, no doubt worried sick about what was going to happen to a boy with no background and no talent for getting along with people—indeed, almost a genius for the reverse—had made me read it, and then quizzed me daily on Dale Carnegie's surefire methods for getting not just along but ahead in the world.

As I walked down the flight deck on some errand a few hours later, Nelson came up alongside me, threw his arm around my shoulder—not done in the navy—and said, "Hey, Al, what's your hometown?" One of Carnegie's basic opening moves. I was thunderstruck. Nelson must surely be a maniac, here in this topsy-turvy world where death and mutilation were likely to be in every strange sound and sight, what influence could anyone possibly have that would be of any use? Who were these "friends" to be won? Where? I could only stare at him. The gods of war love nothing more than irony, and to be so blind to where and what we were was downright dangerous. Inevitably, a few days later two of our planes, one carrying Nelson, went into a cloud in close formation and never came out. Even the wreckage was never seen. They must have collided, thrown into one another by heavy drafts. I used to wonder if Nelson thought of winning friends and influencing people as the plane suddenly split open and spilled him out into the air, down to the water below, down to the bottom.

The course was south-southwest, across the equator, and down to the Southwest Pacific—Australia, New Caledonia, Rabaul, and the Solomon Islands—where the Pacific action had shifted after Midway. This was, by late summer 1942, the farthest reach of the Japanese drive, and it was along the line running from the Solomons to New Guinea that the navy had elected to defend the shipping lanes to Australia and end the Japanese expansion. The marines had gone ashore at Guadalcanal in August, and by the end of that same month the carriers *Enterprise*, *Saratoga*, and *Wasp* had already fought the third of the five great carrier-to-carrier battles of the Pacific war—the Battle of the Eastern Solomons in which a small Japanese carrier was sunk in exchange for very heavy damage to the *Enterprise*. A number of good friends aboard that ship, including Whitey, with his new tooth, and Dallas in the chiefs' mess, were killed at that time. The *Enterprise* limped back to Pearl for repairs.

The *Hornet's* long journey from Pearl Harbor ended at the entrance to the reef outside the harbor of Nouméa, the capital of French Caledonia, and I marveled as we went straight through the narrow passage in the coral, the reef just off both sides, how a trip of thousands of miles could arrive at its destination so precisely. New Caledonia was only semitropical, but it seemed romantic enough from our anchorage out in the windswept bay, with its long mountain chain running down to the beaches and the forests of palms. Ashore, where we went for a brief liberty, Nouméa, was a small French colonial town with a square, a cathedral, a cinema, a few stores, and a rickety racetrack that in time would become only too familiar. There wasn't much of it, but the smells and the architecture seemed genuinely exotic—white plaster and tile roofs. After a few turns around the square, however, and some ice cream made with coconut milk, the sailors crowded back on the dock to catch the next boat back to the ship.

The *Hornet* herself was the biggest attraction in the area. Crowds of sailors who were building the base near Nouméa came out in all kinds of craft to tour the carrier. We were happy to serve as guides—someone different to talk to—and we felt like real heroes compared to these shore-based sailors. When one friendly group told me as they left to be careful not to get sunk, I was quite surprised; the real possibility had never crossed my mind, and I explained quite earnestly to them that a ship this big and powerful could always take care of herself.

At the beginning of September the *Hornet* joined the *Saratoga* and the *Wasp*, patrolling along the eastern Solomons to control the air and keep three Japanese aircraft carriers that had not been at Midway from coming down from Truk and getting at our ships and the marines on Guadalcanal, a name we began to hear for the first time, with the dark tones that have never since left the old Spanish word.

The area was so filled with Japanese submarines that it was soon called Torpedo Junction, and not long after, the *Saratoga* was hit by a single torpedo and retired for repairs. A few days later, up to the north and east of Guadalcanal, we were on routine patrol with the *Wasp* nearby. I had been up all night and had worked through the morning as well, and just after lunch I finally found a cool place in the squadron compartment, several decks down below the hangar deck and well aft. The bunks could not be let down during the day, but lying on the deck with a duct blowing cool air across me, I went off to sleep, only to be waked almost at once by general quarters.

Few things were taken so seriously as going at once to your battle station when general quarters was sounded, but we had been having alarms and going to quarters night and day for a week, with nothing happening. So I decided "to hell with it," for once, pulled a mattress down to conceal me, and went nicely back to sleep, expecting that the drill would be secured in five or at the most ten minutes, and that no one would miss me in the ordnance shack, which was where I was supposed to be. The ship remained deadly quiet, however, and it began to feel eerie down there all alone, and so I got up and made my way through one watertight hatch after another—court-martial offenses—by a back route, unlikely to be observed, until I got to the hangar deck. There I looked out through one of the open metal curtains and about a half-mile away, down on the port side and to the stern, pouring out huge clouds of black smoke was the *Wasp*, hit hard and going down from several torpedoes from a Japanese submarine.

Everyone was so excited that I was able to sneak quietly, much subdued, into the ordnance shack. Later the question actually did come up of where I had been because without my knowing it, I had been put down to fly that day on the antisubmarine patrol that took off when the *Wasp* was hit. It didn't matter—someone else filled in—and I told a story about being slow and getting trapped behind some watertight doors that couldn't be opened. But it was a dramatic lesson, and I never again failed to respond to general quarters, even when the alarm sounded every hour of the day and night for days at a time, which now became the normal way of life, with frequent reports of submarines and sightings of Japanese scout planes.

Unknown new ships began to show up in the task force, like the new battleship *North Carolina*, and antiaircraft cruisers like the *Juneau* and *San Juan*, proof that the American shipyards were really at work. But no new carriers. We were now down to one, the *Hornet*, in the South Pacific, and though the odds were now three Japanese fleet carriers to one, we raided different Japanese bases and made runs to the north toward Truk and then retired south, going into Nouméa sometimes for supplies. To the west, trying to prevent the Japanese navy from reinforcing and supplying the troops on the Canal and other islands in the Solomons, stretching down diagonally from the northwest near New Ireland and the big Japanese base at Rabaul on New Britain to Guadalcanal, the U.S. Navy engaged the Japanese in the most ferocious surface battles of the war: cruisers, destroyers, and torpedo boats, and even once in a while a battleship, against one another in the dark and in the confined waters of "the Slot" between the islands. The Japanese ships and tactics were better, especially at night, and we heard of heavy losses, with grim stories of our own cruisers being unprepared for nighttime battles and firing into one another. "Iron Bottom Bay" became the name for the area between Savo Island and Guadalcanal, where naval gunfire still ruled the ocean, but only at night when the planes from the "Cactus Air Force" on Henderson Field were grounded.

Fear and nervousness began to be constant presences on the ship, tempers grew short, and people gave up any attempt to live a normal life. Sandwiches were the standard food, everyone slept where they could with life jackets and helmets on, the ship was dogged down most of the time, foul smelling, and at general quarters almost constantly. The pilots took to carrying sidearms, .45-caliber Colt automatics in a shoulder holster that would weigh them down if they went into the water but made them feel more secure should they be shot down and drifted ashore on one of the dark little islands that came up from time to time on the horizon. I was sent down to the armory to draw a case of these antiques from the First World War—still beloved by the U.S. services—and then sat in the ordnance shack disassembling them, soaking the parts in a solvent to remove the Cosmoline in which they had been stored a generation earlier for another enemy, reassembling them, and issuing one, plus two clips of ammunition, to any pilot who stopped by to sign for one.

The *Enterprise* had returned from repairs, running at high speed from Pearl in little more than a week, and on the morning of October 26, 1942, off the Santa Cruz Islands, north and east of the Canal, her search planes found the Japanese fleet carriers coming down from their base at Truk in the Caroline Islands to interfere in the continuing battle that was going on between the marines and the Japanese for the possession of the airfield on Guadalcanal. The Japanese fleet was a bit over two hundred miles out, and its scouts found us before we found them. The *Enterprise* planes were mostly committed to the search, and the main attack—dive-bombers, torpedo planes, a few fighters for cover—was delivered by Air Group 8 from the *Hornet*. We worked hard to get the planes gassed and loaded with bombs and a few aerial torpedoes. After Midway everyone was doubtful about torpedoes, but the new TBFs were much faster and more defensible. Some torpedo planes, however, were now used as glide bombers: "glide" since they couldn't take the steep dive of a true dive-bomber but went in at a long low angle and high speed to let the bombs go and then used their speed to get out as fast as possible.

On the *Hornet*, a few miles from the *Enterprise*, the air freshened, as it always did, and the deck vibrated as she turned into the wind and launched the strike group. The planes circled for a time, formed up, and straggled off to the north where a scout plane was broadcasting the location of the enemy fleet, the usual decoy fleet out in front that seemed always to fool our strike groups, the big carriers about sixty miles behind.

Then both American carriers launched a new CAP, took the morning CAP aboard to be refueled, and then sent the planes aloft again instantly to form a maximum fighter protection against what was surely coming. If on a clear sunny day we had spotted the Japanese, their scouts, following the same routines as ours, we knew, had surely found us. In the eerie quiet that falls on a carrier after all its planes have gone off on a strike, everyone lit a cigarette and looked out at the ocean. The moment passed as the ship secured from flight quarters and went to general quarters to prepare for the coming attack, sending all bombs and torpedoes to the magazines, emptying the aviation gasoline lines and filling them with CO_2 to prevent fire. Flash burns from explosions had turned out to cause the heaviest casualties on board ship, and we stuffed our dungarees into our socks, buttoned up our shirt collars and cuffs, put on camphor-impregnated denim flash jackets, smeared any exposed flesh of our hands and faces with a heavy white protective cream, and began to sit and sweat, keeping life jackets and helmets, painted navy blue-gray, nearby.

Our own strike group and the Japanese sighted each other on their way to their targets, but each passed the other by without engaging. I hope they didn't wave, but they may have. Our own fighters thought it their primary job to take the bombers to the target. By now the hard lesson had been learned that sinking the enemy carriers was what counted, not shooting down a few planes, so the Americans flew on to find the Japanese ships, and the Japanese flew on to find the American ships, which they soon did. Earlier, some of the *Enterprise* scouts had found a small Japanese carrier and destroyed its flight deck, without sinking it, but the main force, with the big carriers *Junyo*, *Shokaku*, and *Zuikaku*—the latter two Pearl Harbor carriers— had not been reached as yet.

A little after 0900, the public address system broke the quiet of the ship with an announcement from the bridge. "Enemy aircraft at fifty miles and closing." An unbelievably short time later we heard, "Stand by to repel attack by enemy aircraft," and almost instantly the 5-inch guns located at the corners of the flight deck began firing—bang-bang-bang—in their heavy slow rhythm, not nearly fast enough it seemed to us. These battles developed speedily, and with the five-inchers still firing, the old Navy Yard one-point-ones began going off with their much faster but still deliberate rhythm.

In the ordnance shack, just below the flight deck, we could see nothing, only listen, feel the vibrating steel deck, and slide back and forth with the steep turns of the ship that came in quick succession. When the new 20-

millimeter guns spaced along the catwalks began their continuous rapid firing, we knew the attack had commenced and that the dive-bombers were coming down and the torpedo planes—for the Japanese still used them to deliver with deadly accuracy the big blows—were making their runs at water level. Someone had mounted a .30-caliber machine gun in a railing support just to starboard of the island, and when I heard it clattering away, I knew they must be close. A bomb went off with a great flat bang that shook the ship deep in her bowels where it had penetrated before the delay fuses—contact forward, inertia aft—fired. Then another, and the elevators jumped up in the air and came down, locked, with great bangs.

Then, just up the passageway, past the dive-bomber ready rooms, near the admiral's quarters, there was a huge explosion. A bright red flame came like an express train down the passageway, knocking everything and everybody flat. A Japanese plane, hit, had suicidally crashed the signal bridge and then ricocheted into and through the flight deck just forward of the area where we were sitting. Its bombs rolled around and did not go off, but its gas tanks had exploded. We got up and ran to the other, after, end of the passageway and by a ladder there up onto the flight deck at the after end of the island. There the one-point-one gun crews were down in a bloody mess. Their magazines had been stacked in a circle behind them, and bullets from a strafing plane had caused them to fire at knee level into the gun tubs.

We rushed back down the ladder and stood there hesitating whether to go back up on the flight deck or take our chance below. Two great heavy thuds raised and then dropped the entire ship, torpedoes going home one after another on the starboard side, below the waterline—the death wounds of the ship, though we didn't know it at the time. The *Hornet*, turning at a sharp angle, shook like a dog shaking off water and began to lose speed instantly and list to starboard, which was terrifying, for you were still alive only so long as the speed was up and the ship was answering. You sense it in the soles of your feet, and it began to feel noticeably different at once, sluggish and dull, the rhythm off, and then another delay-fused bomb went through the flight deck just aft, through the hangar deck, to explode with a sharp sound somewhere deep below, followed by an acrid smell and smoke curling up out of a surprisingly small hole. The rudder was now jammed, and as the ship began to turn in circles, all power was lost. The fire hoses stopped putting water on the fires that now were everywhere.

Fire was behind us, and the flight deck was too exposed, so we went down on the hangar deck, already listing sharply to starboard, with the edge of the

October 26, 1942, the Battle of Santa Cruz. Japanese dive-bomber hits the *Hornet*'s signal bridge. It then went through the flight deck and exploded near the place where I was sitting in the ordnance shack. (*Naval Institute Collection*)

deck in the oily seawater that was running into the midships elevator pit. I ran down a long ladder and skidded into the bulkhead, for the steel deck was covered with oil. The forward bulkhead of the hangar deck exploded and the motor and cockpit of a burning Japanese torpedo plane crashed through and fell into the forward elevator pit. Its bomb failed to explode, but its gasoline now caught fire and the deck around the wreck began to glow red.

It had already done tremendous damage when it crashed into the gun sponsons on the bow of the ship, probably after the pilot was killed while making his run on the port bow, or perhaps he was an early kamikaze, carried away with the sight of the enemy ship so close and filled with battle will to obliterate it. One of the compartments he hit on his way through the ship was a blanket storage, and his plane had set the blankets afire and scattered them burning and smoldering the length of the hangar deck. The navy had fine white blankets with blue bands—these were officers' blankets—and the smell of burning wool mixed with fuel oil remains my dominant sense impression of the day.

The guns stopped firing. The first strike was over, but by now the ship was dead in the water, and you had to be careful, so steep was the angle of the hangar deck, not to slide on the oily surface out one of the openings and into the water on the starboard side where the torpedoes had hit below the waterline, flooding the compartments below. The island and bridge hung menacingly out on the starboard side, seeming about to topple over and take the ship with them. There was fire forward where the plane had crashed through, the deck was red with heat, and several bomb holes in the oily deck were pouring out smoke. Among the burning and smoldering blankets dotted about the deck were bodies, some terribly burned, others dismembered, some appearing unharmed. The burns were the worst to see, huge blisters oozing fluid, the tight charred smelly flesh, the member sometimes projecting as if straining for some final grotesque sexual act. A place not to linger, but there was now all-hands work to be done here.

Damage control managed to correct the list somewhat, but power and electricity were still gone, and fire fighting had to go on by hand with buckets and a fire-retardant powder. The cruiser *Northampton* came up to tow the *Hornet*, sending over her steel towing cable to be attached to the anchor chain after the anchor was unshackled. The huge water-filled ship actually began to move, until the cable broke on the *Northampton* end and dropped in the water. There was no power on the *Hornet* capstan to haul it in, so it was dropped.

A second attempt was made using a two-inch steel cable that was stowed in the well of the midships elevator pit of the *Hornet,* an ominously dark and slippery place by now, partly under water. This cable, hundreds of feet long and tremendously heavy, had to be uncoiled and passed, like some huge stiff greasy snake, by hand to the bow of the ship where it was secured before being sent over to the *Northampton.* Everyone in the area was rounded up for this job, and we formed a solid line up the hangar deck, slipping and sliding, heaving in rhythm, trying to move the dead weight of this steel boa constrictor. From time to time the guns would go off again, and everyone dropped the cable and took cover. But after a while we did manage to get the cable forward, and a boat from the cruiser picked up the end to begin towing preparations again.

No planes would ever land or take off from the *Hornet* again, and the air divisions, my own squadron included, provided free hands for the grim task of gathering the dead and wounded. I worked for a time on the flight deck helping to carry the injured crewmen from the gun mounts and the bridge to a corner on the high port side forward where the doctors had set up a hospital and rigged some awnings to protect the wounded from the brilliant sun that never stopped shining all day.

As I started back across the flight deck, the guns began firing again as a single dive-bomber made a run on us. I lay flat on the deck, covering as much of my body as possible with my tin hat, trying to work my way into it, and thinking for the first time that I was likely to die, and resenting it, feeling that at nineteen I really hadn't had a chance to do most of the things people do, and vowing to do them if I survived. From that moment to this, life has continued to seem a gift—overtime in a way—and all the more enjoyable for it.

The bomb missed, and I ran to shelter in a compartment in the island where hundreds of other sweating frightened men were huddled behind thin steel bulkheads. By now the ship felt terribly heavy. Power had not come back on and nothing worked any longer.

All this time the *Enterprise* had remained visible in the distance while hiding under a squall from the Japanese planes, but about noon she too came under attack. The antiaircraft shells made the sky black and the ship twisted and turned, but in the end she caught three bombs, but no torpedoes, and continued to operate her flight deck. Our strike groups, having heavily damaged one of the Japanese carriers, *Shokaku,* but not sunk her, were returning. The *Enterprise* would take her own planes aboard and as many of the *Hornet*'s as possible, but the others would have to land in the water, their crews picked up by the destroyers serving as plane guards. So now the *Enterprise* picked up speed and moved away to the north, preparing to land planes. On her deck the pilots taking off were shown a famous message chalked on a board, "Proceed without *Hornet*."

As she became smaller and then went hull down on the horizon, the war moved away from us, and with an awful feeling of loneliness we turned to the business of survival. Three destroyers moved in alongside us on the high port side, only a few yards away, with their masts and yards swaying wildly back and forth as they tried to maintain station in the swell while passing hoses over to fight the fires aboard the carrier. The *Hornet* did not move at all, but the lighter destroyers, pitching and rolling, from time to time would crash against us with a terrible clang. The rigging would catch in the catwalk above and tear away when they rolled back, and their radar and fire control were being battered and broken in the process.

Lines were passed across, and when possible we began to pull the wounded over to the destroyer, some in wire stretchers, others sitting in a boatswain's chair. Speed was crucial, since we expected to be attacked again, and the destroyer had to cut loose if that happened. Men stood by the connecting lines with axes. Those of us on the lines pulling the chairs and stretchers over to the destroyer ran down the oily hangar deck with the line, and then ran up again, hoping to God that we wouldn't slip and go crashing into some piece of unyielding iron or go skidding out into the oily water coming in on the starboard side. Fires still burned forward, bodies lay around the deck, no time or need to move them. Below, the work went on to try to restore some power, but the Japanese torpedoes were real killers, in contrast to our own inept weapons, and there were no flickering lights, which would have indicated that the dynamos were starting up again.

The ship was now the business of the ship's crew, particularly the engineers and the damage control groups, and the Airedales had nothing to do. We were assembled again on that ghoulish hangar deck, where I asked an officer if the smoking lamp was lit. Under stress, he was annoyed by the question, and there was a danger of fire, so he snarled that surely a sailor could go one day in his life without smoking. I muttered something about "What if it's the last day?" and got away with it in the confusion of the moment.

I decided that things did not look good, and that we were probably going to abandon ship, so it was time to prepare. I could not bear to leave all those bright new guns that I had polished so nicely that morning, so I made my way up to the ordnance shack, picked one out, and put it in a sack, just in case. Encouraged by my own bravado, I then did something extremely foolish and dangerous. I made my way down through several hatches and dark decks to my locker. The water sloshed ominously on the low sides of the compartments, but my locker was on the high, dry side of the ship, and I had no trouble and stupidly felt no fear of the ship rolling over and sinking. A pillowcase held my basic gear, including a suit of whites in case we went some place where there was liberty, but a diary I had been keeping for some time—contrary to regulations—was reluctantly left behind. In a moment I was back again on the hangar deck, the envy of all my friends for having salvaged some clothes, answering muster. The Airedales were to be taken off since they served no useful purpose on the ship any longer.

About 1500 the destroyer USS *Hughes*, one of the fire-fighting destroyers alongside, stretched cargo nets between the two decks. The *Hornet* sat heavy and still, filled with the seawater that would take her down, but the *Hughes* rolled and pitched. When she came into the *Hornet* she crushed the net and anything in it between the sides of the two ships. Trial and error, after a few people got caught, taught the right way to do it. The trick was to jump just as the *Hughes* began to roll out, being careful that your foot landed on one of the tightening ropes, and not on the holes between, for there wasn't time to recover and make your way slowly up a loosening net. If you did it right you landed on the rope and its stretch would pop you like a trampoline onto the deck of the *Hughes* and into the arms of several of her crew. Carrying my pillowcase filled with my contraband pistol and my liberty whites, I leaped for my life and made it with a great bound of exhilaration. Tricky, but better than going into the oily water where anything could happen.

At the best of times in war a destroyer is a small and crowded ship, and as about four hundred additional men squeezed aboard, every space above and below deck was filled to the point where literally it was difficult to move. Just as I got aboard, another Japanese strike, launched from their surviving carriers, roared in. The *Hughes* cut her lines, pulled away at high speed, and started firing her antiaircraft guns. Looking for a place with some protection, I crawled under the mount of the after 5-inch gun, which swung around above me, the bolts holding the gun to the swiveling mount missing me by what seemed no more than a quarter of an inch. The firing directly above and the clang of the hot shell as it came out of the breech was too much for me, and I crawled out thinking what a real mess it was going to be if a plane came in strafing, with the deck absolutely filled with people who couldn't move without going over the side.

In a moment one did, just as I forced my way into an after deckhouse already crammed with sailors trying to cover up their heads. The enormous power the ship was turning up gave a speed of about forty knots and forced the stern deep in the water, forming a huge stern wave that made it impossible to see anything aft except the wall of water. The destroyer was not hit, but it seemed as if we were all going to go down because the incoming Japanese torpedo planes made their run on the *Hornet* from behind the *Hughes*, zooming along on the wave tops and then juking up and down at the last moment. The carrier took more bombs and one additional torpedo, making her death certain. In the same attack the *Northampton*, trying to avoid a spread of torpedoes aimed at her, dropped the last towing cable, ending that slim hope of saving the *Hornet*.

Fortunately, no plane came near us, and the destroyer's officers began sorting us out, making sure that each bunk was filled in six-hour shifts, putting the injured below deck near the sick bay, arranging for each group to appoint one man to come to the galley to draw food twice a day. The Torpedo Six ordnance gang, about seven or eight of us by now, found ourselves aft on the starboard side, sitting on a narrow deck with our backs to the after deckhouse bulkhead and our feet outboard to the rail resting in the scupper. It was an uncomfortably wet place at high speed, but there was, just above our heads, a rail welded to the bulkhead to which it was possible to tie yourself, even when hanging onto a full pillowcase, which I began to curse but refused to give up.

The very long day of October 26, which I always celebrate privately, was drawing toward sunset. We were still circling the *Hornet*, but as it became clear that no power could be raised and that the effort to tow was finished, the command was given to abandon ship, and the crew began to go over the side on ropes and to jump into the oily waters. There was no room for any more survivors on the *Hughes*, so as the other ships moved in to pick up the rest of the crew, the *Hughes* turned south and began withdrawing. The Battle of Santa Cruz was over, and sitting on the deck, cold and exhausted, looking back at a tropical sunset with the smoking carrier sitting there at an odd, lumpy angle, I for the first time considered the possibility that we might lose the war. It had been such a big and powerful ship, and yet only a few hits in a brief space of time had been enough to finish her. Then too it was already apparent, as it would be crystal clear after we knew all that went on that day, that the American navy had fought ineffectively.

But the navy would be back, and even in going down the *Hornet* was tougher than we thought. Still later that evening our own destroyers went back to finish her off with torpedoes, but once again the American torpedoes failed. Some missed, some failed to explode, and those that hit did not sink her. The destroyers then turned their 5-inch guns on her, starting more fires, but still, after several hundred rounds, they failed to put her down. By then the Japanese surface fleet was getting close—they were still trying to force a surface battle—and the American destroyers withdrew, leaving the scene of the battle and the hulk of the *Hornet* to the victors in the battle. She was too far gone to be salvaged, though, and a few of the superb Japanese long-lance torpedoes at last blew the bottom out of her, and she went down in more than three miles of water to where she must still be sitting, as beautiful and proud as ever.

It seemed the final irony that our torpedoes and guns couldn't even sink our own ship, that we needed the Japanese and their weapons to finally put us down.

SEVEN

Wandering

It was my job to go below and get the food for the ordnance gang, and Murphy, in one of his fits of wryness, gave me his chief's hat to wear, insisting that by wearing it I could go to the head of the serving line. Since I looked about sixteen years old, in a navy where chiefs were still old and grizzled, it was a grotesque joke, but I played my part to the hilt, crashing the line, giving abrupt orders about the corned beef sandwiches and coffee—which was all we had—and never dropping a smile. It must have amused others too because they let me get away with it, even asked admiring questions about how I had made chief at such a young age, to which I responded with tall tales of skill and daring against the enemy. Cut off from his moosemilk, Murph must have been having ferocious withdrawal symptoms, for he sat all day with his ordnanceman's red-cloth helmet buckled under his chin, his brown fear-sharpened face with its huge hooked nose looking out to sea like some naval muse of tragedy. Sitting beside him with the oversize chief's cap coming down over my ears, I supplied the comic balance.

It took only one night on that exposed passageway on the ship's open side, wet and waked all night by waves, to make it absolutely necessary to find some less-exposed place on the crowded deck. Getting below was impossible. In the morning we began to scrunch forward to the well deck where the torpedo tubes were located. A little pushing and shoving, some curses here and there, and we found some room under the inverted vee where the two flues from the boilers came up at an angle and joined about five feet above the deck to form the destroyer's single smokestack. The deck here was hot from the boilers beneath, which was fine for a time, and good for drying out, but it got too hot all too soon. We adapted by laying down cardboard and sleeping on the deck as long as we could take it, then climbing out to cool off in any odd perch for a time, and then diving back into the heat and the sleep. Wherever you were you tied yourself to something before going to sleep since it was easy at any time to get washed off a destroyer deck. We were all pretty numb, which helped, and grateful to be alive under any conditions, which helped even more. By the end of the fourth day we were just hanging on when the *Hughes* came to the entrance to the New Caledonia reef and took us to the anchorage off Nouméa.

Small craft took us off at once. Trucks met us in the dark, blackout being enforced, and bumped up the island to dump us off at some tents where we were told to draw a folding army cot, mattress, and mosquito net and find a place to sleep. Used to the insect-free life aboard ship, we didn't secure the mosquito nets properly, and by the morning my feet were so swollen from bites that I couldn't get my shoes on. We were on the edge of a salt marsh, between the lagoon and some high bare mountains. There was an Australian brigade, wonderfully jolly, camped on one side of us, and a New Zealand brigade, terribly dour, on the other, there to defend the island. Someone thought that the nearly three thousand men from the *Hornet* would make dandy support troops in a pinch.

It seemed as if it might come to that one day when two barges were sighted by patrol craft and identified as Japanese carriers leading an invasion force. But fortunately the Japanese never got around to invading New Caledonia, and we passed our time swimming, gambling, and sneaking out over the mountains to pester farmers in isolated farmhouses—"*Avez vous vin?*" A few bottles of sour wine mixed nicely with juice squeezed from the lemons growing all around us to make a wonderful party. We invited some Australians, but not New Zealanders, and they regaled us with stories of what stuffed shirts the New Zealanders were.

The *Hornet* crew was too well trained to be left on the beach for long in a time of shortage of trained personnel, and within a few days the ship's crew was sent off to the States for leave and reassignment. Air squadrons were needed in the South Pacific, however, and each of the four *Hornet* squadrons was divided in two. One group, made up of those who had been overseas longest, was sent home. The second group was used to form small new squadrons. Having been overseas only a year, I fell into the second group, and we all gathered around Murph and Moyle, Berto, Vanderhoof, and others to see them off on the trucks and tell them to have one for us in Dago.

The rest of us, an astonishingly young group, were reunited with six of our old pilots and given some new planes to form a small squadron to be sent up to the Canal, where the fighting got worse every day. Our flying field was

The grandstand at the Nouméa racetrack that served as ready room, club, ordnance shack, engine repair shop, sleeping quarters, and anything else necessary, in November 1942, after the *Hornet* sank and Air Group 8 was put on the beach in New Caledonia.

the old colonial French racetrack, with a rickety wooden grandstand for quarters and workshops. It was a pleasant enough place, except that every time a plane turned up its engine, it blew dust over everything, including the guns and engines we had just cleaned. But life in the grandstand, with its benches for beds and tables, was casual and relaxed, the weather warm and sunny, and we could wander into town whenever there was no work to be done, so long as we weren't out after sundown and curfew. It was nothing like the famous novel and musical that was made about it, *South Pacific*, by James Michener, but island life was nice, and an occasional ride in a plane gave a view of the long island stretching out for a hundred miles, mountains down the center, white beaches and a fine coral reef extending around the entire coast.

It didn't last long, though, and one night after sundown we were told to load the planes with all the spare equipment, to pack our gear—there had been an issue of basic clothing—and to go down to the dock where, at the end of the quiet Nouméan street, hundreds of sailors were lined up in the dark, out to the end of the wharf. The water was full of small squid, and in the kind of weird humor thought funny by young men at war, the sailors on the edge of the dock would reach in the water, pick up a squid, and throw it up in the air to let it land on someone's head or face. Not knowing what the clammy thing was, standing close packed in absolute darkness and unable to move far, already nervous and uncertain, it was real psychological torture, and the furious reaction came close to breaking out in a riot.

In time, excruciatingly slow time, small craft took us out to the USS *Kittyhawk*, a strange old tub used before the war for hauling boxcars loaded with bananas from Central America. The middle third of the main deck was open on top and down the sides so that a crane could lift the boxcars onto railroad tracks embedded in a cement deck, where they could then be rolled fore or aft. The *Kittyhawk* was now a plane transport, not a banana transport, and the decks were loaded with planes of all kind, including our own, destined for various islands. The ship was overloaded, and we were to sleep on the deck with the rails, getting under the upper deck when the rain squalls came, as they often did. Fine, but as we moved in among the planes looking for a place to sleep, dogs started snarling and barking frenziedly. All along the outer bulkheads were chained the most ferocious bunch of dogs, German shepherds and Dobermans, I have ever gotten to know. These were guard dogs going to Guadalcanal to smell out Japanese soldiers—God help them—in the jungle. Their chains were short enough to keep these excitable creatures from getting at one another, but any human other than their handlers—they seemed to be hiding somewhere—who stumbled into their arc was in big trouble.

By daylight we were beginning to wallow along, north between two chains of islands that formed the New Hebrides group, leading up from the south to Guadalcanal. It was rainy and steamy hot, and the islands, low and dark and close, had an ominous look that made you vow not to go near them if you could help it. Food was hard to get and not worth it when you did, but you could buy candy at the ship's store, and a group of us bought a huge bag of small Hershey bars. A new member of the ordnance gang taught three of us to play whist—not bridge but old-fashioned, eighteenth-century whist— and we sat all day long playing it, for money, of course, eating chocolate bars and jumping at the sudden snap of canine teeth whenever the player sitting with his back to the dogs raised his hand and reached back to throw his winning card, particularly the ace of clubs, down to take the trick. The dogs sat looking at us rather coolly, while we tried to avoid eye contact.

By the next day we were at Espíritu Santo, the largest and northernmost of the New Hebrides. Here we learned that our small torpedo squadron was not going to the Canal but, with a pickup group of fighters, would become the air group of an escort carrier, the USS *Nassau*, anchored off the island. The *Nassau* was one of the small carriers that had been built in a hurry in large numbers by adding a flight deck on to the hull of a large freighter, putting in one small elevator aft, rising from the hangar deck to the flight deck, and adding a tiny island about halfway forward on the starboard side for a bridge and air-control quarters. Planes were launched by catapult, the deck not being long enough to fly off and the ship incapable of getting up enough speed to help out very much, twelve or thirteen knots being about tops, and not sustainable for long.

After the great fleet carriers like the *Enterprise* and *Hornet*, the *Nassau* seemed ludicrously small and dangerous. Our eyes lit at once on the torpedoes locked in racks running up the side of the hangar deck, the only place aboard ship to put them, probably, but terrifyingly exposed to any accident or explosion. The *Nassau* and her type were intended for antisubmarine patrol in the Atlantic and would never have been sent into the naval battles in the Pacific if it had not been that after the end of the *Hornet* we were now down to one damaged carrier, the *Enterprise*. If the Japanese made an all-out assault on the Canal, anything that could launch planes would be thrown into the battle.

It was a cramped and awkward ship, and the squadron was in no mood to make the best of it. We were naval snobs, used to the big ships and the smartness of the prewar navy, and everything about this little tub, manned with reserves, and some dregs of the regular navy, offended our sense of propriety. We sat about playing cards and bitching endlessly about everything aboard. At anchor the weather was stifling and the humidity overwhelming. We were crammed in a tiny compartment designed for half as many men, and the ship had no ship's store, barbershop, or "gedunk locker" (ice cream counter). The food was dreadful.

Our planes—the TBFs and the little fighter planes, the F4Fs, the early versions that were used instead of later models on the escort carriers to save room—were kept ashore on a muddy field where we went daily to work and to talk to the army, navy, and marine pilots and crewmen who were flying into and out of the Canal daily. We worried that we would be used on some kind of suicide mission to save the Canal if the Japanese navy came down in force.

Guadalcanal came to have a mythic status as the place of death as stories were told along the flight line of desperate land battles just at the end of the runway mats on Henderson Field, of planes taking off and dropping their bombs almost immediately on Japanese ships coming down the Slot, of nighttime shellings by Japanese battleships, and of our own ships firing into one another in wild confusion. We ate it up, half longing to go to the mysterious place and half hoping to stay in reserve.

There was only waiting. Christmas and New Year's Day came and went. The natives were happy to climb a coconut tree and throw the nuts down and show us how to open them by putting a sharpened stick in the ground and driving the nut on it, breaking open the husk. But this amusement had its limits. Mail finally arrived, including Christmas packages sent months before, leaking melted soap and chocolate—everything melted on Espíritu Santo—smelling of endless quantities of after-shave lotion and writing paper. A huge mound of unopened packages belonging to the members of the squadron who had already gone home was piled up in a small compartment where it was raided by anyone in need of a razor or reading matter. Shaving lotion seemed to be in every package, and we were all wondrously fragrant, though we had begun to look like a bunch of pirates.

The intelligence officer of the squadron had been a notable pain in the ass, and one way of lifting flat spirits was to root through the deteriorating pile of Christmas packages until you found one—there were surprisingly many—addressed to Ensign B. and then to loot it with many foul jokes about B.'s ancestors, person, and practices. I carried for years a pigskin toilet kit some loving aunt had sent him, and felt every time I used it some modest revenge on a foolish but dangerous man who had actually threatened to have me shot for falling asleep leaning against a plane one night on the *Hornet* while standing guard over the planes on a closed and stifling hangar deck in a temperature over one hundred degrees, after working for more than twenty-four hours.

By the end of January the Japanese in the Solomons had begun to break, and they abandoned their efforts to supply and reinforce their troops on the Canal and the lower Solomons, pulling back to Bougainville and to their base at Rabaul. The Japanese advance that had begun at Pearl Harbor had finally been halted, and stopgap ships like the *Nassau* were no longer needed so close to the battle lines. Our planes came aboard by lighter, the anchor came up, and we chugged eastward to a new anchorage off the northern coast of the main island of Fiji.

There was no port here, and so the ship was anchored, quite alone, off-shore, surrounded by a torpedo net that retained the ship's garbage and the sewage from the heads quite efficiently. Uninviting, yes, but as the heat built up, swimming was allowed, and even the most fastidious went booming off the deck, hoping to avoid the floating turds below. After a while, like many things, it didn't much matter, until the snakes arrived. Some kind of white-and-black-striped coral snake that swam upright in the water, moving its tail back and forth in a most sinister fashion. There was debate about whether it was poisonous; no one really seemed to know.

A group of us were soon sent ashore to service our planes, located at an army air base. We could eat in the mess hall there, but we seldom did for it was a long walk—about five miles—from where our tents were pitched in a grove of cool trees. There was nothing to drink, but the natives soon found us and brought us rice and pineapples fresh from the fields where they worked.

The Fijian natives were a noble, intensely black race of people, generous and with a fine sense of humor. They were also delighted to see us and for a few cents a day to clean out the tents, wash clothes, provide fresh pineapple centers for breakfast, and take us at night to native dances in little one-room schoolhouses, where we sat on mats, joined in the songs, watched the intricate dances by men and women, and drank the local drink made from some pounded and fermented root, which seemed never to have any effect of any kind. But it gave you something to drink and helped the spirit of merriment. From time to time army military police in Jeeps would stop to make sure that no servicemen were mixing with the natives. A whistle from the native guards would alert us, and we would run out into the fields to hide among the cane or pineapples until the police had left.

Strong loyalties were built up in a short time between the Fijians and us, involving the exchange of gifts: a woven mat for a pair of shorts, a copy of the lyrics of the lovely Fijian song "Ise Lei" for a cigarette lighter. From time to time we would go to the nearby town of Nani, inhabited almost entirely by Indians, the descendants of the laborers who had been brought by the British to work in the cane fields in the late nineteenth century. The Indians were merchants who then mostly beat silver coins into jewelry and ran small grocery and dry goods shops. The town was dusty and hot, and since we had no money, not having been paid in a long time, we were looked on with great suspicion. We responded by identifying with the Fijians, a care-free warrior people who delighted in filling us full of stories about the wicked and unnatural ways of the Indians. We agreed happily, ate more pineapple, drank more kava, and sang the endless verses of "Ise lei, nona nogurawa," or something that I remember that way. At night we would sit out and watch the stars and exchange stories with the Fijians about the way things are.

Occasionally, one of us would go back to the ship to shower and to buy cigarettes and candy bars, both of which the Fijians loved. On one of these errands I got caught for shore patrol. In the old days, each division on a ship furnished so many shore patrolmen to keep order in each liberty party and to see that everyone got back aboard without wrecking anything. The idea was to take care of the men and protect the citizenry from them, not to represent law and order. Not a popular job, but I was stuck, issued an SP brassard, a nightstick, a pair of canvas leggings, and a .45 automatic in a holster attached to a web belt buckled around the waist. Someone had discovered an old hotel up in the hills, about three miles from the shore up a steep red-dirt road, where cane whiskey was to be had. Worried about the crew going crazy from the heat and the boredom, the executive officer decided to let a liberty party go each day for a couple of hours to see the countryside and to drink.

The day began badly, with a light rain, and worsened as the liberty boat came alongside, an old battered fifty-foot motor launch used ordinarily for hauling garbage and not cleaned for its new purpose. In the heat, the smell got down in the stomach right away, auguring worse things to come. The liberty party looked fine as usual—brightly washed, carefully pressed whites, shiny black shoes, clean caps and neat neckerchiefs—and, there being no gangway, the sailors scampered smartly down the metal ladder that hung from the quarterdeck down to the motor launch below. Nothing looks more innocent or reassures more about human nature than sailors lined up to go on liberty. Few things look less reassuring than when they return, and this was going to be a monumental demonstration of that truth.

As the boat moved away toward the shore, the rain began to come down more heavily and bits of leftover garbage began to slosh around inside the launch. No dock, so the launch ran aground, and the sailors jumped over the side and frolicked like clean white lambs up the road that was already beginning to turn to oozy red mud and to wash away in deep gullies. The rain began to get serious and tropical, the brims of white hats were turned down to shed the downpour, and the liberty party began to come apart. In the mud, rain, banana trees, and heavy foliage, the jungle began to break down the discipline, of which I, along with four other SPs, was the representative. Some of the squirrellier sailors began to roll in the mud and disappear into the jungle alongside the road. Where they were going, God alone knew. Back to nature, I thought, as, soaking wet with sweat and rain, I bird-dogged them through the underbrush, trying to keep them moving up the mountain.

A large percentage of the old navy was alcoholic, getting blotto whenever they could, and we were driving some of these world-class sponges toward a long bar in an old wooden resort hotel that sold some of the rawest popskull on the planet. The first real drink after months of imbibing shaving lotion and paint strained through a loaf of bread relaxed them a bit. There was even some momentary real laughter here and there as one group stood under the eaves leaking rain while the others fought their way to the bar, a dollar a shot, and new groups elbowed their way through. With the second drink people began to stand on their dignity, ancient quarrels broke forth to new mutinies, and hard words began to be heard. Purposely, no officers had accompanied this fete, and the SPs had been told that when things began to get rough, to head the rowdies back down the mountain. That time arrived with the third drink, as fighting began right down in the mud with kicks and eye gouging. The kanak who ran the bar offered the SPs a drink as we started back, and though it was absolutely against the rules, we knew we were going to need it and took it gratefully.

The sailors had to be clubbed away from the bar, and straggling, slipping, and falling they made their way cursing down the mountain, stopping from time to time only to fight a bit more. The SPs were like sheepdogs fanned out in a semicircle at the rear keeping everyone on the move. In my sector a bitter quarrel began between a drunken Jew and an even drunker black mess attendant. The old navy was, among other things, covertly anti-Semitic and openly racist. The few Jews in the navy always had a hard time of it, I thought, but usually rolled with the punches. There were many blacks in the navy, but they were segregated in menial jobs as officers' mess attendants, cooks, and pantrymen. It was a lily-white navy that never gave its racism a thought, and I was about to get a lesson in its strange effects. It seemed to me mad for two people who both obviously had such a bad time of it to turn on one another. But they tore at one another—crazed by the cane whiskey and a lot of accumulated frustrations—like furious animals. I separated them time and time again, warned them, exhorted them morally, in my innocence, only to find them once more down in the mud. It seemed to me that they ought to turn on their tormentors, like me, but, no, they raged at one another.

At last we got them to the launch, the rain still pouring, and the liberty party—covered with filth and mud, drunk and disorderly—put off from shore to go alongside the USS *Nassau*. Since there was only the one swaying ladder up to the quarterdeck, where stood the august officer-of-the-deck in his starched whites, getting the drunks to go up was a real problem. There is nothing a drunken sailor likes better than to make a scene when returning from liberty. "Quarterdecking" was the technical term for acting a lot drunker than you were. This particular scene offered lots of opportunities for quarterdecking: dropping off the ladder into the water, to be fished out with a boat hook by one of the small boat crews, or vomiting on the deck as close to the officer-of-the-deck as possible.

But my two were the stars. We had separated them in the launch and kept them that way, sending the mess attendant up the ladder first. But as he got onto the deck, with me following hard after him, instead of turning aft and saluting the flag and the officer-of-the-deck, with a wild cry he picked up the big wooden box in which liberty cards were to be deposited and, raising it high over his head, hurled it down the ladder, grazing my ear, at the Jew who was shouting obscenities at him from down below in the boat. That finished it. The really tough masters-at-arms who were on duty on the quarterdeck clubbed the mess attendant down and hauled him off in an instant lest his outstretched body offend the majesty of the navy. Those of us who were SPs that day were only amateur policemen, and we would not have reported the trouble at all, as long as we all got back in one piece, but the masters-at-arms on ship were a rough sort and their ability to keep the peace had been questioned in the full face of authority. I never heard what the punishments were, but I think they must have been awful.

Scuttlebutt began to say that we were going back to the States. The remnants of Torpedo Squadron Six were transferred to the *Copahee*. It seemed impossible at first, but sometime in late February the nets were taken away, the anchor came up, and the ship got under way for San Diego. Somewhere south of Pago Pago, as we stared at Samoa in the distance, one of the ship's two propellers gave out. Steering was difficult thereafter, and the already maddeningly slow standard speed of ten knots dropped off to six at once, and the coast of California receded farther into the distance.

> Day after day, day after day,
>   We stuck, nor breath nor motion;
> As idle as a painted ship
>   Upon a painted ocean.

When I read Coleridge's lines from *The Ancient Mariner* years later, memories of the USS *Copahee* on the vast Pacific—sun blazing down, nothing else in sight, the horizon unmoving, proceeding from Fiji to San Diego at six knots, clumping away, out of balance with one screw turning—filled in the picture. Tedium was monstrous, and trying to relieve it for even a moment, I got into a poker game over my head, attempted to run a bluff on a master card shark, and lost the hundred dollars I had saved up for the thirty-day leave we would get in San Diego. Despair and ennui struggled for mastery, and a borrowed fifty cents got me into a penny-ante game made up of those who had lost all in various bigger games run throughout the ship by the sharks getting together a stake for the fleshpots of America. A run of luck raised my capital to over eighty cents, fifty of which I used to buy a ticket in one of the anchor pools that various entrepreneurs were running.

There are in an anchor pool a set number of chances, each marked with a time. The winner is the owner of the chance marked with the exact time (always officially noted in the ship's log) that the shackle is knocked out to release the anchor chain or, if the ship is tying up at a dock, that the monkey fist on the first heaving line strikes the dock. The pool I had bought into had 720 chances, one for each minute in a twelve-hour period—A.M. or P.M. made no difference—which meant that those who ran the pool had collected three hundred sixty dollars, of which they would give the winner three hundred, keeping a profit of sixty for their efforts. Fair enough, but with only one chance in 720, I forgot about it as the ship at last in late March came in sight of the coast, rounded Point Hard On, and worked up to a dock on the western end of the Naval Air Station. Looking at the Naval Training Station across the channel, it seemed a lifetime away. The monkey fist sailed out in the air and landed with a clunk on the dock. "1024, first line across" came the announcement over the loudspeaker. I went down to get my seabag since the Airedales were to be transferred to some old buildings in the park at the San Diego Zoo, the other animals having gone some-

where else, when it hit me. I scrabbled to find my ticket, and there it was—
"1024!"

Few joys have exceeded that moment in my life. To get off ship, to go on leave, and to be rich, all at once. Three hundred dollars was a lot of money in those days, but now I had to move fast to make sure that I found the oper- ators of the pool before they left the ship with all the money, or hid out somewhere aboard until I was locked up in the zoo and couldn't get back. Such guile was not unknown in naval life, and all my suspicions were aroused, but the sailor who ran this pool was an honest man, hunting all over the ship for me, greeting me with real pleasure and counting out the money in old tired tens, fives, twos and ones, a great wad I couldn't get in my wallet.

A happy, comic ending to a long grim sixteen months of war, a real lift to the spirit, a feeling that things would work out.

EIGHT

Stateside

The desert, sagebrush, and mountains that had been so familiar two years before now seemed strange and bleak. The train was crowded, and as I looked out the window, I saw the cold March wind blow the snow ahead of it and the drifts lying here and there on the dry brown earth and the soft gray-green of the sage. I had expected my return home to be nothing but pleasure, but the land seemed hostile after the tropics, and I was cold in my new set of tailor-made blues and peacoat. My anchor-pool fortune had been partly spent on the Hamilton wristwatch I had always wanted—the last of prewar production still in the jewelry store—and on a tightly fitted gabardine dress blue uniform: bell bottoms, zipper up the side of the skin-tight blouse, a dragon sewn in gold and green thread on the satin lining inside the front flap of the pants secured with thirteen buttons.

The leave had nearly ended in the Union Station in Los Angeles. I had worn my issue dress blues with the loose blouse, the bottom tied halfway up my chest and folded over to form a roomy pouch in which I had placed the .45 Colt automatic I was smuggling home. It was too risky, I thought, to put it in my seabag, which was searched when I left the base, so along with a hundred rounds of ammunition—some tracer, some ball, some incendiary, the works, all for hunting rabbits!—it went into my blouse, making a grotesque lump. All went well until, in the middle of that huge waiting room, I bent over and the gun, fully assembled, went sliding out the vee neck of the blouse, onto the floor with an awful clang, and across the slippery surface at high speed. There were shore patrolmen all over the place, and visions of life in the naval prison at Mare Island flashed before my eyes. I think that others must have seen the gun, but because it was the last thing anyone expected to see on the floor of Union Station, no one recognized it for what it was, as with what seemed nightmarish slowness, step by agonizing

Home on leave, March 1943, in the tailor-made uniform—tight waist, bell bottoms, gold dragon sewn in the thirteen-buttoned flap lining of the pants—bought with some of the money I won in the anchor pool.

step, I ran after it, hunched over to conceal it, and slipped it back in my blouse.

The train pulled into Rawlins in the middle of the night, the temperature well below zero, and we drove, my stepfather and I, the forty miles back to Saratoga, with nothing really to say, over the frozen land. By then—the middle of the war—most of the other young men were gone from the town, and I found myself the hero of the moment, invited to speak at the Lions Club on the progress of the war. As if I had any notion of how it was going, but I was flattered to be asked. The father of the marine who had been killed at Wake broke down in tears and wanted me to explain why we had not gone to his son's rescue. I cried too and explained that we had wanted to, as if the crew had had something to say about it, but that it just hadn't been possible that time, but we surely would win in the end and avenge old Bobby. Everyone insisted on buying me drinks at the Rustic Bar, where I developed a taste for whiskey sours—it took months to get my stomach deacidified again—and a willingness to tell sea stories and talk naval strategy. All this lionizing was new to me—before the war I had not been one of the more prominent citizens of even so small a town as Saratoga, Wyoming, population 680—but I took to it at once, casting off all restraints of modesty and good sense.

But it was the girls that really surprised me. My appeal to the other sex had always been rather limited, and though I was a willing servant of Venus, none more so, I never had had a regular girlfriend before the war and customarily had gone home after dances swearing never to go again and be humiliated by girls, plain as well as pretty, who found excuses to avoid dancing with me. But now there were no other men, and the uniform really did, as I had heard rumored overseas, seem to work some kind of magic. Girls who would never speak to me before were now willing to dally and to charm. Most myths are just that, myths, but the connection between sex and war must have some truth in it, for chastity seemed to have been cast aside in the Rocky Mountains for the duration. It was all terribly crude, awkward, drunken fumblings on car seats, but it was hot and full of life, joyously restorative and reassuring, a reminder that, even if clumsily managed, intense pleasure exists in a world that offers a lot of dullness and pain. Sex and war really initiate us into society, and I began to feel more a part of what really goes on, not merely an observer.

The past still threatened and could only be faced and then forgotten as much as possible. My mother's grave in the town cemetery on the dry hill overlooking the alkali lake just outside town was already collapsing and pocked with gopher holes. To one side, partly hidden by a rise, were the gray weather-beaten rodeo grounds, and to the other was the town dump, spotted here and there with rusting cars from the 1920s with unfamiliar names like White, Jordan, Stanley, and Star. It was right, in the grotesque way life has of being symbolic, for she was another wreck from that era. Her family, Fletchers and Macmillans, lived for a hundred years on land in south Georgia taken from the Indians and distributed in land lotteries to Revolutionary War soldiers in the early 1800s. Life was rural: small farms, cotton and corn, Primitive Baptist churches, a few slaves until the Civil War, large families.

The post–World War I generation to which she, born in 1900, belonged was the first to leave the land, and with a little education, she married a soldier, moved to town, went to Florida, lost the money from the sale of her father's farm in the land boom, divorced with a child, and began a long American wandering—Chicago, Memphis, a ranch in Wyoming.

My mother remarried, became a Catholic, put a bright face on it all, but she was the first generation of really rootless modern Americans, moving restlessly by car about the country, emancipated socially and intellectually to a modest degree, but lost really, without any supporting society or family and without the familiarity with this alienated condition that makes it possible to face it directly and do what can be done with it. Lostness has been the understood state of later generations of Depression and war, but not really of my mother's, and she had few defenses against it.

People had changed in Saratoga, but not the land. The mountains were still there as they always were and will be, the streams of melted snow ran down from them to the Platte River, which ran down to the Missouri, which went into the Mississippi and then to the Gulf of Mexico. I was staying in town but went up on one sunny day with Vernon Swanson, a neighbor, to the ranch. The snow was still four feet deep down in the canyon, and we went on snowshoes, exhilarated by the clear air and the brilliant sun. Down in the canyon the snow was melting, and the creek was running rapidly under the ice. Beyond the canyon walls the huge peak of Vulcan Mountain began to loom up above us, heavy and dark green, gradually blocking out the sun as we went farther up the canyon. By the time we reached the cabins of the ranch where I had grown up and my mother had killed herself, the sense of freedom and ease had gone, replaced by a feeling of heaviness dominated by mountains, cold snow, and gloomy pines.

The war and its great battles had seemed more important than mere country mountains and streams, and I thought I had outgrown these ruralities. But now nature reasserted its authority, reminding me of a durability and monumentality that made human affairs, no matter how world-shaking, trivial and passing. The mountain spoke too of its complete indifference to human ways of reckoning and feeling. Nature goes its way, and if mankind wants to tag along, fine, but our schemes and hopes do not scratch the reality of nature. Vernon and I drank whiskey from a clear pint bottle and then threw it up into the air, where it flashed in the light, turning over and over, and shot at it until we broke it, but this bravado only made us feel smaller, and after picking up the glass, we were glad to go down the canyon again, up on the ridge, and out of the shadow, if not the presence, of the mountain.

Thirty days pass like all other time, and the transient barracks at the North Island Naval Air Station was dark and noisy. Someone in the bunk next to me kept a small rattlesnake that he had found out at the end of one of the runways and amused himself by putting on a glove and making the young snake rattle and strike. Terrified of snakes, but ashamed to show how much, I avoided the area any way I could and was relieved when I was assigned to the torpedo squadron of a new Air Group 6 that was forming at North Island. Most of the members of the old squadron were assigned to shore duty at the Assembly and Repair unit at North Island, but the new squadrons needed a core of veterans and, perhaps because I was younger than most, I was chosen to go back to sea. I was actually glad to return overseas, there was by then something flat, even squalid, about life ashore, lying about your age to drink in cheap bars, sitting in dull movies, always broke and borrowing a dollar for liberty, shirking work, no sense of unity or purpose among the people you bunked with.

To get back to the squadron was different. There were a few old friends—Moyle was now the chief of the ordnance gang—and the new pilots and men were excited about going overseas and impressed by those of us who had already been there. New squadrons are busy places, with an enormous amount of detail and hard work. For the ordnance gang this meant endless loading of practice bombs for mock bombing runs and rigging tow targets for gunnery practice. The bullets of each plane firing on the target were dipped in a different-colored paint, and afterwards we sat around and counted the number of blue, yellow, red, green, and black holes.

One of the new sailors in the squadron was a man who became a close friend, Dick Boone. (He and I went to New York after the war for a time, sharing an apartment in the Village while I attended Columbia for a term and he went to the Neighborhood Playhouse, a famous method-acting school.) He was several years older than I and had been educated at Stanford, but we hit it off, and I went on several overnight liberties with him, riding the train to Los Angeles and staying with his family in Glendale. It was the first I had seen of a well-to-do family and home. It was, I learned in time, as troubled as most, but I was overwhelmed by its comfort and pleasant ways. The Boones welcomed me warmly, and I soon fell madly in love with the seventeen-year-old daughter, Betty. This they did not welcome so warmly since I was about as bad a prospect as a son-in-law in every way as could be imagined. But their uneasiness never changed their kind attitude

Some members of the reconstituted Torpedo Six in a San Diego bar in May 1943. Dick Boone—later a movie star—is standing to the left, then Gaffney, Kernan, and Dutscher, who lost his whiskey on Maui. Since servicemen were forbidden to own a camera, these bar pictures—a dollar a copy—were taken by scantily-clad, pretty girls and were usually the only photographs we had to remember people and times by.

toward me. The father was a wealthy lawyer who had laid in a stock of fine whiskey at the beginning of the war. He was generous with it, and I thought it was the height of luxury to ride the night train back with Dick from Los Angeles to San Diego at the end of a weekend liberty, drinking scotch—new to my unseasoned palate—from a dimpled Haig and Haig Pinch bottle.

The war was moving on fast—new carriers, new squadrons—and by late May, Air Group 6, commanded by Lt. Comdr. Edward O'Hare, was loaded aboard ship and sent off to finish training on one of the Hawaiian Islands, Maui. O'Hare, known as Butch, was a hero of the early war, having shot down five Japanese planes on one day when flying off the *Lexington* in the Rabaul raid a year earlier. His father had invented the mechanical rabbit chased by race dogs. O'Hare Field in Chicago was named for him after Butch's death a few months later, in which I was to be closely involved.

We landed at Pearl Harbor and then on a bright clear day, with the wind blowing hard, went with all our gear on a huge cement barge towed by a tug down past the leper colony on Molokai to land at Maui and the new navy training field there. Most of Maui was brown and dry, and the field was built below the huge bare extinct volcano, Haleakala, that had formed the island. It dominated the landscape, and we often flew down into its dead crater, lush now with flowers and greenery. The airfield was rudimentary: short landing strips, earth revetments for the planes, standard wooden barracks for the men, cottages for the officers. We were here to learn to work and fly together, and the days were long and busy. The nights too, since night flying in formation was frequent, but somehow it still managed to seem the most luxurious place I remember in the war.

The climate was perfect, sun and breeze, the discipline relaxed, and there was a beer garden for once. A palm roof over a few rough board tables and benches, but we were allowed two cans of beer a day, and they tasted like nectar at the end of a long hot day's work. We sat and talked, drinking the cold beer with the late afternoon breeze coming through the sides of the hut. I don't remember a word that was said there, but I can still feel how pleasant and agreeable it was.

Not all was idyllic, for we were inclined to trouble. I amused myself one evening by climbing the revetments in a Jeep and ended by getting high centered on top of one and having to be towed off. The officers got a bottle of whiskey a week, and one pilot who didn't drink gave a bottle to his radioman, Dutscher, who hoarded it in his locker and refused to give us any or to drink it himself. This seemed downright inhuman and worthy of the most savage revenge. One night when he was in the air, we carried Dutscher's locker out onto the field where we shot the lock off and, leaving the locker there, took the bottle of whiskey off to the empty beer hut to drink it with great satisfaction. Dutscher was extremely unpleasant about the whole business after he returned and found his locker missing, but he gradually came around and ended by saying that he only really minded that we hadn't saved him a drink, the bottle being empty by the time he found us.

On another occasion word got around that one of the officers was keeping a kootch, a local whore, in a cabin down in the bushes, but that she was bored with the officer and was seeking virile young enlisted men. With a few beers behind us it seemed a fine idea to go down and visit her. She was less over-joyed to see us than we had been led to believe, but was persuaded to show us her famous tattoo of a mouse disappearing into her pubic hair and in the end was so pleased with our admiration that she dispensed favors to all, for a price. Whether she really had any relationship with any of our officers I never learned, but to think so made the experience somehow more satisfactory.

The skipper of the torpedo squadron was a fine man named John Phillips, and one day he announced that he was looking for a new gunner. Moyle, loyal to the survivors of the old squadron, recommended me for the job, and after a few trial weeks I settled down to being the lead gunner in the squadron. No one minded, or even brought the matter up, but I had not a bit of training for the job. I knew about the machine guns and had a general familiarity with the planes, but of aerial gunnery—the deflection angles of two planes coming at each other from odd directions and speeds, and so on—I knew not a thing except what I had learned about hunting in Wyoming. But I was honored with the job, and it never occurred to me that there were some skills in which I was dangerously deficient. We all picked up what we needed as we went along.

The lead gunner of the second division, fiercely mustached Buck Varner, former driver of the Los Angeles fire chief's car, and I made bets on which division would hit the tow-sleeve target most often. I was never more delighted than the day I persuaded Phillips to move in close to the sleeve and fly parallel with it at exactly the same speed. With this setup you couldn't miss, and the first division blew the target to pieces, leaving huge smears of red, the color on the tip of our bullets, on the ragged remnant. Phillips didn't know what was going on, but stood laughing when we landed and laid the first and second division targets on the tarmac in front of the ready shack. Buck Varner couldn't believe his eyes. For every hit his division had made there were fifty of ours. I played the game out for all it was worth but didn't take his money. Everyone had a beer and the squadron laughed for days.

Gambling was a way of life in the navy, and everything we did was made more interesting by wagering on it. The TBF was a high- and low-level bomber as well as a torpedo plane and was equipped with one of the famous Norden bombsights of which it was always said, wrongly, that they could put a bomb in a pickle barrel from twenty thousand feet! Each gunner was also a bombardier, by virtue of his job, not his training. The radioman who sat down in the tunnel would get up in the turret while the gunner got down in the tunnel seat, opened the bomb bay doors, turned on the sight in front of him, and looked down through the bay to line up on a target far below. In practice, only the lead plane of the division used the sight, while the other planes released their bombs when they saw the lead plane drop. The whole system, depending on variable winds and temperatures, was a rickety, unworkable arrangement, but I had a certain feel for the sight and had great luck combining its functions with a lot of guesswork, raining down practice bombs and sometimes big yellow five-hundred-pounders on the bombing range.

We bombers practiced in a vast hangar where an automated mobile box, looking something like a metal shoe box with a target pinned to the top, started from one corner. Riding a framework vehicle, steered by one man while the bomber sat about ten feet above and in front with the sight, you began tracking the slow-moving box. This simulated bombing plane would stalk the moving box and when directly above it would, using a series of delay timers, drop a plumb bob, the point of which would make a mark in the target. The mark closest to center collected the pool for the day. Varner pulled his mustache, wept, and swore I cheated, but day after day I walked away with the loot, acquiring a reputation as a master bomber, which I never tested in action since it was obvious to the admirals that high-level bombing with TBFs was a waste of time. We had the sights only because the army had them and the navy didn't want to be left behind.

Flying with the squadron commander had its attractions. The relationship was formal, and the radioman, a telephone lineman from Reno named Sullivan, and I called him captain and asked permission to fire the guns and secure the hatches as if we were on a battleship. But Phillips was a genial man given to flying off for the day to have lunch in Honolulu or to fly over the great volcano on the main island of Hawaii, landing at the little Somerset Maugham tropical town of Hilo, where we wandered about while he borrowed a Jeep and toured the island. We never missed a chance on the way to Honolulu to fly low over the leper colony on the long spit of land with the cliff at the end on Molokai. The lepers never failed to come out either to wave or to shake their fists at us, we never knew which.

There were endless training missions in which the squadron took off, assembled, flew to a target together, bombed it, and then formed up again and flew home. Woe be to the pilot who didn't join up in time or fly a tight formation. One poor fellow, known as Dilbert after a cartoon character used in flight training posters who did everything wrong, spent two hours one bright moonlight night trying to find the other seventeen planes of the squadron as we flew back and forth over the great dead volcano. Finally, Phillips had had it and after asking Dilbert for his location, told him to stay right there and we would join up on him. We did, and Ensign Dilbert went back to "Uncle Sugar" the next day for further training.

NINE

Night Fighters

By late October the idyll was over. The USS *Lexington* (CV 16), a new carrier replacing the old *Lexington* lost in the Coral Sea in May of the previous year, was cruising off the coast, and we flew out to her, practicing attacks for several days. Returning to Maui, we packed our gear on ship and flew the planes to Ford Island. Pearl Harbor was filled with new ships. The losses of the first year of the war were beginning to be made good for us, not for the Japanese, and the great drive across the central Pacific that would end in Tokyo Bay less than two years later was beginning. On November 10, Air Group 6 flew out to the *Enterprise* for the attack on the Japanese bases on the Gilbert Islands scheduled for the end of November. After the ship left Pearl and we had landed aboard, the yeoman handed me orders directing me to report to San Francisco for training as a pilot. I had applied in Maui, having always wanted to fly, but had expected nothing to happen from the brief physical and written exams I took. Now the orders to report to San Francisco and to flight training were there, but there was no way back until the cruise was over, and I would go through some of the most remarkable events of my life during the next month with the constant thought that if the orders had come one day earlier I would have missed it all.

A huge task force of carriers, cruisers, destroyers, and transports assembled to the south of the Hawaiian Islands and sailed down the central Pacific to the Japanese-held Gilbert Islands, where we were to land troops on Betio (or Tarawa), with its landing field, and, slightly to the north, Makin Island. The *Enterprise* was assigned to provide air support for the army's Makin landing. The marines were to take Tarawa. Both islands were pounded with naval gunfire, and then on D-1 day and on the morning of the landing, carrier planes went in against any targets still standing. On the morning of November 20 the transports unloaded the troops into the assault boats.

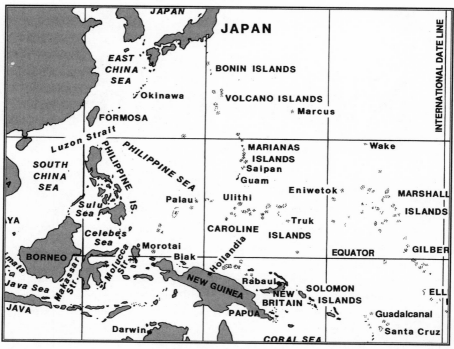

The navy was beginning its drive across the western Pacific.

Phillips's plane provided a perfect seat to see the entire show, flying liaison back and forth not far above the atoll, blue water, circular coral reef, white beaches, and coconut palm groves, reporting on the progress of the assault to the command ship. Tarawa was a bloody mess from the beginning, when the assault boats hung up on the reef, but at Makin the attack proceeded like a movie. The cruisers and destroyers blasted away, squadron after squadron of planes flew in strafing and dropping bombs, a long line of Higgins boats moved up to the southern hammerhead of the island. As the first soldiers rushed up the beach, hundreds of cheering natives rose up out of the brush and broken trees and rushed down to greet them with open arms. The Japanese garrison had retreated earlier up the handle of the island, but the natives had stayed behind, eager to see Americans and be rid of the Japanese. It had been assumed that nothing could live through the working over the assault area had been given, but few of the natives were hurt, and as they ran happily down the beach our fearsome weapons of war began to look less than effective.

The same lesson was taught again later in the day as we circled around, watching a group of torpedo bombers loaded with old 16-inch armor-piercing battleship shells that had been converted to aerial bombs with a delay fuse, trying to skip bomb a wrecked ship half out of the water off On Chong's Wharf. The wharf, built years ago by some Chinese trader, was a wobbly structure sticking out into the lagoon and was about the only thing with or worthy of a name on the whole atoll. The coastal trader that had sunk off it in some long-forgotten storm had been occupied by the Japanese, who used it as a pillbox from which to fire machine guns at our soldiers after they had passed it and landed with their supplies on the beach. Skip bombing was a new and briefly used technique in which you didn't try to hit the target directly but came in on a line with it, about a hundred feet above the water, and dropped the bomb at an angle so that it hit the water and then skipped up in the air and landed on the target. Bang! Utter Destruction!

Why this was thought a better way of destroying the target than hitting it directly was no more obvious than why two-thousand-pound armor-piercing shells designed for World War I battleships should be converted to aerial bombs to be exploded on a rusty old wreck that you could kick a hole in. But so it was decreed, and as we circled, plane after plane came in, dropped its bomb in the sparkling clear shallow water, only to have it hit the sandy bottom, leap up, and skip clean over the ship to land with a big explosion on the beach side, or to skip high up in the air and explode with a flash that threatened the plane that had just dropped it.

It was an exercise in the kind of futility that wars are made for, but as we turned in a wide circle over the island, feeling smugly superior to all the nonsense below, we were reminded that we were by no means out of war's confusion. There was a ping, only a little one, and a sudden smell of the gasoline that was trickling into the tunnel where Sullivan and an observer along for the ride, an intelligence officer, were seated. The bomb bay had been filled with a huge auxiliary gas tank to allow us to fly liaison all day long without having to land to refuel, but the auxiliary tank had no self-sealing lining, and when some irritated Japanese gunner drew a bead on us, flying slowly and, no doubt, infuriatingly, overhead, a lucky hit pierced the tank and filled the plane with fumes that could explode with a single spark. The intelligence officer later wrote himself into the dispatches and recommended himself for a medal—which Phillips instantly killed—for saving the plane by pouring coffee from a thermos on the gas, thus, he said, holding down the fumes and preventing an explosion. He did pour the coffee out—Sullivan and I watched him do it and both decided he had gone mad with fear and begun to act irrationally—but what saved us from blowing up was good luck. No one was smoking at the time, and the pilot quickly opened the bomb bay doors and dropped the big green auxiliary tank on the Japanese lines, hoping we had hit the soldier who had hit us. The gas in the plane evaporated quickly and, nearly out of fuel, we flew back to the *Enterprise* to land, refuel, and take off, without our coffee-pouring observer, for another afternoon of observing and reporting.

There was little resistance on Makin, the blood all being spilled a few miles to the south in the really terrible fighting on Tarawa. But the army advanced cautiously, and we flew far ahead of the troops up the atoll, a few hundred feet above the blue water and the sandy beaches, weaving in and out across the reef and the island, looking for any signs of Japanese support troops or new entrenchments. Mostly we saw only natives fishing, who waved happily. But as we flew back to On Chong's Wharf some Japanese soldier let rip with his machine gun, blowing some pieces off the plane, which then went into a dive that dropped my stomach right out my bottom. "Prepare to crash, prepare to crash," Phillips shouted over the intercom, and then the plane lifted a little. "I think I can hold it with the tabs."

We were okay for the moment, holding flying altitude not far above the water, but the problem was not solved. One of the bullets had come through the fuselage in back of the radioman and cut the steel-wire elevator control cable that connected the pilot's stick to the elevators. The tabs are small inserts in the elevator, controlled separately, that can be rolled up or down to keep the plane in a climb or descent without the pilot having to maintain constant pressure on the elevators. Now they compensated for the down pressure on the loose elevator and kept us in something like steady flight. But landing on a carrier is tricky business, requiring drum-tight control cables to provide hair-trigger responses. So it looked like a water landing alongside the carrier was the best we could hope for, and such landings, while they worked often, were always high risk, particularly with faulty controls. Too many things to go wrong, a bump on the head, a jammed hatch, the plane sinks instantly!

Radioman Sullivan got on the intercom to say that he thought he could join the two raveled ends of the elevator control cable using his telephone

The splice in the elevator cable that Radioman Sullivan, a former telephone lineman in Reno, made after it was severed by a Japanese machine gun from the ground on Makin, November 1943. The .50-caliber shell along the top of the cable was used as a lever to take up the slack in the splice. The hole in the frame shows the angle at which the bullet entered. Sullivan's parachute harness, which he had taken off to work on the cable, hangs on the flare chute.

linesman's skills, which he proceeded to do, standing up in the tunnel below the opening of my gun turret, where I sat looking down with great interest between my legs. A lot of time passed, with everyone literally sweating through their khaki flight suits, but finally the splice was made, and though the cable hung down with a lot of slack, Phillips could make the plane go up and down again using his stick. But that, he explained over the intercom, wasn't good enough for any kind of landing, on the water or the deck. The cable had to be taut and respond more or less instantly to his control. Sullivan, a little over five feet tall and able to walk upright in the tunnel, was a very ingenious and a very courageous fellow, and he said that he thought he could work some cord we were carrying into both sides of the splice and then twist a .50-caliber bullet into the weave and by turning it again and again, as in a tourniquet, take up a lot of the slack. This too worked after a long time, and Phillips finally declared himself willing to try a deck landing on the *Enterprise*.

The *Enterprise* was less sure. They didn't want the flight deck fouled with a wreck at that point, and though they finally agreed, they made us wait for another eternity, during which time Phillips tried out another idea on Sullivan. "What I am going to need at certain points in the approach and landing is a lot of movement in a hurry, and the slack cable will move the elevator too slowly. On the landing approach, could you stand in the tunnel, holding onto the bullet that is providing the tension in the cable, and when I say 'NOW' over the intercom, give the cable an instant manual assist in whichever direction it is moving?" Landing on a carrier is rough at the best of times, requiring us to be seated and buckled up; but Sullivan agreed, stood upright in the tunnel, and pulled and pushed on the cable at the critical points.

Phillips was a master carrier pilot, and he flew the crippled plane carefully around its lurching approach. Every movement was slow and exaggerated and likely to spin off into disaster. Sullivan hung on to the bullet for dear life, locked his feet on whatever purchase he could get, and in the end, when Phillips gave the final "NOW," pulled the cable forward with all his might to stall the plane out and drop it on deck, getting thrown into the radio forward as the arresting wire caught the tailhook and the plane stopped short. (A picture of the life-saving splice and the bullet hole appears on the preceding page.)

It had been an exhaustingly long day, long enough by far, but that night a formation of Japanese bombers flew down from the Marshall Islands, just to the north, to look for our carriers in the darkness. They never found us, but, all lights extinguished, we remained at general quarters all night. I was sitting on the flight deck, my legs hanging over into the catwalk alongside, when in the complicated maneuvering another great warship came rushing straight at us, a huge black mass, only to turn at what seemed the last moment and pass by us to port, so close that I could actually call out to the sailors standing helplessly on her deck.

The Japanese had big airfields on Kwajalein and the little islets Roi and Namur—several hundred miles to the north in the Marshalls—out of which they were flying medium bombers, Bettys, loaded with torpedoes, down to Tarawa and the American fleet, hoping to sink a carrier or two. It was decided on the *Enterprise* to do something about them, and Adm. Arthur Radford, commanding Task Force 50.2, in consultation with Butch O'Hare and Phillips, devised the first night-fighter operation off carriers, code-named "Black Panther." A few small airborne radar sets had been issued to the fleet the year before, but they were not yet in general use. Primitive instruments, with a small green screen about five by seven inches, they had a sweeping arm that briefly lit up with bogies as it crossed their location—terribly difficult to read—with a maximum range of about ten miles and precise only much closer. Still, having seen nothing like them before, they impressed us mightily. When lost, you could find your way back to a ship with one of these, instead of flying on into the empty ocean until you ran out of gas. Sets had been installed in two of our torpedo planes by a specialist, Lt. (junior grade) Hazen Rand, who had worked in the development of the airborne naval radar sets at M.I.T. After a crash course in operating the rear gun, Rand replaced Sullivan in our tunnel for the Black Panther operation.

The idea was simple in plan, more complex in operation. A radar-equipped TBF with a belly tank would be launched at dusk and would stay up all night. Then, when the bogies appeared later, fighters would be launched from the *Enterprise,* and all could land at daybreak, thus avoiding a night landing, for which neither pilots nor ship was yet trained. Once the fighters were in the air, the fighter director officer, using the ship's radar and the new VHF (Very High Frequency) radio, which the Japanese, it was thought, could not pick up, would vector two fighters and the torpedo plane with radar to a point near the bogies. There the more lightly gunned TBF would, using its radar, lead the two heavily armed fighter planes (with six wing-mounted .50-calibers each) to where they could see the exhausts of the Japanese planes, who did not use flame suppressors at that time, and then break away, leaving the fighters to complete the attack.

This plan was later modified by O'Hare and Phillips in a manner explained by Admiral Radford in his letter of December 4 to the Commander Air Force, Pacific Fleet.

The [new] plan consisted of launching one TBF-1C and two F6F-3 airplanes. These planes were to proceed ahead of the ship and effect a rendezvous. After rendezvous, the Fighter Director Officer was to vector this section to the nearest or largest group of enemy planes. An attempt was to be made to place our night fighter group on the quarter of the enemy formation distant about one to two miles. From this point the TBF pilot with the assistance of his radar would home on the enemy planes, attempting to close on the rear of their formation. When within sight of the enemy planes and when directed by the TBF pilot, the fighters would close the range and open fire.

The crew of 6-T-1 on November 26, 1943, the day before Butch O'Hare was killed in a night-fighter action off the *Enterprise*. Sullivan, who did not fly that night, sits on the wing between Lieutenant Commander Phillips (right), the squadron commander, killed at Truk in 1944, and Lieutenant (junior grade) Hazen Rand, who operated the airborne radar and was wounded in the tunnel of the plane that night. I am to the far left. The sharpened features, particularly the noses, of everyone in the picture are characteristic of people in a state of controlled fear.

It started like this, but it did not finish according to the official scenario.

Bogies appeared on the ship's radar screen about 0300 on the morning of November 24, and two night-fighter groups, each consisting of a torpedo plane and two fighters, were sent up. It was a most confusing night. We never joined up effectively, and when we did get into some kind of formation, the ship's radar couldn't seem to get us in an attack position on the Bettys, and our own plane radar located nothing. The other TBF was piloted by Lt. John McInerny, famous as a pilot in Fighting 8 at the Battle of Midway who had dared to break formation and fly up alongside the squadron commander and point to his gas gauge to show that the squadron was passing the point of no return. Buck Varner was in McInerny's turret. Their plane developed engine trouble and had to land early. The rest of us, disappointed, straggled back aboard about 0800.

About 0500, while we were circling, looking for targets, there was a huge flash of light off to the east, like the sun rising, which we later learned was the escort carrier *Liscombe Bay* blowing up when hit by a Japanese submarine torpedo. She was a light ship, like the *Nassau*, with pitifully little protection, and everything in her—gasoline, bombs, torpedoes—blew up at once. She went down instantly, with the loss of more than six hundred men. Our fears about the old *Nassau* when we first saw her at Espíritu Santo had not been exaggerated.

The next day, the battle being pretty much over at Makin, Phillips, Rand, and I flew down to Tarawa to familiarize ourselves with its airfield in case we had to make an emergency landing there after one of the Black Panther flights. The smoldering fight was still going on in the midst of dreadful devastation. The landing field was clear—though it looked a decidedly unpromising place to land—but the burned and gutted landing craft were still on the reef far from shore where they had hung up and the marines had gotten out with their weapons and waded ashore in neck-deep water. The bodies still floated in the tide and lay bloated on the sand. All the trees on the island were twisted and piled up in great rubbish heaps.

On the night of the twenty-fifth, when the usual flight of Bettys appeared, we sat the evening out. One snooper passed a few hundred feet over the ship, so close we could see his exhausts. The *Enterprise* did not open fire in order to avoid revealing our position. This was all spooky stuff, and by now the crew was nervous and jumpy. When I went below, one of them began shouting at me that it was the Airedales' responsibility to be up there in the night defending the ship, which seemed irrational to me. Let him go up there and defend the ship if it meant so much to him; I was quite content to idle about the deck and take my chances with the rest. A brief fight bled off a lot of repressed feelings.

The rest of the Bettys circled out about twenty miles, dropping a string of flares. The battleship *North Carolina* opened up with her antiaircraft guns in a startling explosion of light and shot down one, possibly two probers.

Then, on the night of the twenty-sixth, the new night-fighting scheme was put into action, but using only one section. One of the fighters was to be flown by Butch O'Hare and the other by his wingman from Fighting Squadron Two (VF-2), Ens. Warren Skon. The torpedo plane was inevitably flown by Phillips as squadron commander of VT-6. Lifetime naval careers were made for officers at places like this. Rand was in the tunnel again, while I remained, somewhat unsure about all this, in the turret. The belly tank was gone—too dangerous, and it made the plane sluggish. The fighters and the torpedo plane were to go off together, early in the evening if the Japanese appeared then, and—here was a big risk—we would all have to land on the carrier deck in darkness, without lights. The barely secured landing field at Tarawa had been requested to receive us if we could not get back aboard the carrier.

Japanese snoopers were already in probing the fleet before sunset, and fighters from the *Belleau Wood* shot down one Betty. Sitting in the ready room under the flight deck, we wore red goggles to keep from being blind when we went into the dark. The only enlisted man in the group, which was ominous, I was excited, but not having any idea what a makeshift, untried business it all was, like most things in war, no matter how often practiced— and this had not been practiced at all—I had no unusual worries. As dusk was falling, the public address system told us that a large number of Bettys had been picked up by radar closing on the ships.

A few moments later came that stirring command, "Pilots, man your planes," and the two fighter pilots, Phillips, Rand, and I made our way up to the flight deck and into our planes. I had checked and double-checked all the guns on the torpedo plane: the .30-caliber in the tunnel, the two fifties in the wings, and especially the .50-caliber Browning machine gun in the turret, making sure that the two one-hundred-round cans of ammunition I had—one in the gun, and one secured to the bulkhead below in the tunnel—were fully loaded with perfectly belted ammunition so that there would be no jams at a bad time. The belts were heavy with tracer—one tracer, one armor piercing, one tracer, one incendiary—in order to see where the stream of fire was going in the night. A great mistake, it turned out, since the light from too many tracers blinded me in the darkness. In the turret I checked the intercom, pulled up the armor plate that locked me in with an ominous click, and turned on the black-hooded gun sight, with its lighted orange concentric circles, just behind the bulletproof plate glass in front of me, while the engine turned up and was tested.

The two fighters went off first, at 1800, fired from the catapult, and disappeared into the distance, small diminishing blue lights just visible from their exhaust flares. The fighter director officer at once vectored them out toward the Bettys without the TBF. We went off heavily next. Looking from the backward-facing turret, I could see the huge black deck rise above us and feel

Torpedo planes forming up above the carrier on way to the attack. Turret and tunnel, with the port on the side and the rear gun below, stood out on the TBF. (*Naval Institute Collection*)

the tug of the waves below. But the engine at full power pulled us up and away, and as the wheels and flaps came up we gained altitude in the darkness and began to move away from the white wakes and bow waves of the task force while waiting for the fighters to join up on our wings.

Right away it began to get difficult in the turret in unexpected ways. The pilot has instruments, particularly an artificial horizon, to tell him whether he is flying level or not and an altimeter to tell him whether he is climbing or diving. The man in the tunnel didn't care since he was enclosed in a black box oriented on the green radar screen. But in the turret you have no instruments. You stare out into the dark night, and after a time you don't know up from down. The first few turns are okay, but then disorientation begins. A flicker of light could be a star in the sky or a ship on the ocean or another plane coming at you on a fast angle. As long as the changes are not too abrupt and frequent, the seat of your pants gives you a sense of where you are, but a few rapid changes and panic begins to flutter around the edges.

From the beginning the fighters were far ahead of us, vectored out by the fighter director officer, against explicit orders to keep the night-fighter group together, to catch a snooper before dark closed in. Though we cut corners everywhere on the vectors called out by the fighter director officer, we dropped farther and farther behind. Since we depended on the fighters for firepower I assumed that once we lost them for good we would go back to the ship. Aft of the ships a string of red flares, from twenty to thirty, went off. Here and there some yellowish float lights had also been dropped to mark rendezvous points, and it was near these points that we later found the enemy.

But Phillips was an aggressive naval aviator, and after a time he decided to strike out for himself. We flew about for a time while the fighter director officer tried to get all our planes together, but still no fighters. Then Rand called out that he had a contact. Four, five, ten, then twelve. Two parallel rows of six Bettys each. We swung in behind them, and Rand began calling out the range: three miles, two, one, a thousand yards. Then, at two hundred yards, the pilot confirmed, "I have them in sight. Attacking."

This seemed madness to me, a lightly armed, clumsy, slow torpedo plane attacking twelve bombers in a tight mutually supporting formation, each with five guns—front, rear, top, two in the waist—but nobody asked for a vote, and the plane banked up and to port, then swung in high on an angle toward the rear Betty in the starboard line. The two .50-calibers in the wings felt like they were tearing the plane apart.

It all developed so fast that training took over from thinking. As we tilted up and away from the firing run on the first plane, I could look back and see the surprised enemy opening up from his top turret, his blister gun, and his tail, the heaviest and most accurate fire coming from the 20-mm. in the tail. Fire flared out at his wing root, where the gas tanks were, and I began firing at the flames. He blew up all at once. A long trail of fire went down and down into the blackness of the ocean below, where it kept on burning, a red smear on the black water.

The Japanese were totally confused. Night fighters off carriers were as unknown to them as they were to us, and the night was filled with so many tracer streams it was impossible for them to tell where the attacking plane was. In their excitement the Japanese gunners were firing into their own planes in the opposite line. By now, I too was in trouble. The turret .50-

caliber, its muzzle less than three feet from my eyes, spewed a flare of burning gases, all the more for the extra tracer, despite a flash suppressor around the muzzle of the gun, which in the darkness made it impossible for me to see the illuminated concentric circles of the gun sight. As long as I was seated I was blinded each time I fired. The only thing to do was to unbuckle my safety belt and crouch on my seat, trying to get my eyes high enough to see over the muzzle flare and fire down the line of tracer into the Bettys, illuminated by their firing guns and their engine exhausts. It didn't work very well, I still could hardly see, but it partly worked, and without being aware that I was doing so, I remained in a crouched position, my head bent over and forward to fit inside the rounded turret, for the remainder of the flight, about two hours, except for two trips into the tunnel below.

As we pulled away from the first kill, the fighter director officer vectored us to other Bettys, and our own radar once again brought us to within visual range of the dark cigar shapes, their exhaust flares burning blue on either side. Just as Phillips went into his firing run, O'Hare, who had seen the first plane burning on the water, called us and ordered the torpedo pilot to turn on his red recognition light so that they could join up and share in the kill. Phillips replied that he was in a firing run and did not want to alert the enemy but that he would blink the light a few times.

The light told the Betty that something was out there, and it began evasive maneuvers, opening up on us as it did so, but Phillips followed closely, and after a long burst the deadly fire showed again in the gas tanks where the wings joined the fuselage.

In Phillips's own words from the official Action Report of VT-6:

> The Avenger opened fire in the right turn at about 200 yards. After firing a good long burst (40 to 50 rounds estimated) the Betty started to burn and continued down and struck the water at about 1000 yards. The Betty left a trail of burning gas about 300 yards on the water and continued to burn as did the other one. It appeared from the attitude of this Betty that it may have been under control when it hit the water.

The Japanese firing was disorganized but not entirely harmless. We turned away from the burning plane and started into a firing run on a third. I fired back into the second plane as it glided down toward the water to crash and burn. Just then, Rand called out on the intercom. "I'm hit."

"Where?"

"In the foot. My boot has filled with blood. I don't know how bad it is, but I have put a tourniquet above the ankle."

"Are you in pain?"

"Yes."

"Too much to go on working the radar?"

"I don't know. I'll try."

"Kernan, go down and see what you can do."

I unlatched the armor plate below me and crawled down in the bucketing plane to sit on the green aluminum bench beside Rand. A pale, thin-faced man anyway, his face in the ghoulish green light of the radar screen was now a skull. A single bullet had come through the plane just forward of the armor on the floor where his foot was braced while he peered into the radar scope, and it had torn off the side of his shoe and foot. It wasn't a mortal wound, unless he bled to death, but it was sure a painful mess. I called Phillips on the intercom. "Shall I give him an injection of morphine?" (We carried Syrettes in the medical kit.) The answer shocked me. "No, we will need the radar again." The logic was obvious, though I didn't think Rand was going to do much more work that night.

I took the opportunity of being in the tunnel to change the ammunition can for the turret gun, a terrible job hunched over in close quarters, the plane rising and falling rapidly, trying to shove a long can weighing about a hundred pounds one minute and ten the next up into a narrow slot. Each time I would get it nearly up to where the retaining latch could catch it, the plane would suddenly rise, and the can and I would go down to the deck or be flung against one of the bulkheads, trying all the time not to step on Rand, sitting there with his teeth gritted tight, or slip in his blood.

Finally the ammo can clicked into place and I jumped back into the turret, glad to get out of the confined tunnel, dark and bloody. We had by this time lost the Japanese planes, but a lone Betty drifted under our tail and I got off a few rounds. Phillips, true to form, began searching again. In my heart I wasn't as sure I wanted to find them as he was. The radar was our only chance, but Rand picked up no blips in any direction. He was making heavy going of it by that time and not functioning well, though trying gamely. We were now circling at some distance from the carrier, and I became increasingly disoriented. The second of the two Bettys that had crashed was burning in a long smear of gasoline on the water, and as we turned in the pitch black, I thought the ocean was the sky and the light from the burning plane another plane turning in, in a long curve for a run on us. I called out on the intercom that it was attacking and requested permission—even here this was still the battleship navy—to begin firing. Phillips, using his instruments, put me right side up again.

The ship's radar could see both us and the fighters, and the fighter director officer was trying to move us together. At this point Phillips—at O'Hare's request—turned on our running lights, and the fighters, all lighted up themselves like Christmas trees, slid suddenly in, coming down across our tail from below and aft, O'Hare on our starboard side wing one or two hundred feet away, somewhat below, Skon on the port, bright blue in the flare of their exhausts, six guns jutting out of their wings, quite scary. Canopy back, goggles up, yellow Mae West, khaki shirt, and helmet, seated aggressively forward, riding the plane hard, looking like the tough Medal of Honor recipient, American Ace he was, Butch O'Hare's face was sharply illuminated by his canopy light for one brief last moment.

Amazingly, some of the combat reports of the Japanese 752 Air Group, fifteen of the Bettys that were attacking Task Force 50.2 that night, survive to tell of losing three planes and of sinking two carriers and one battleship! The distinguished naval historian John B. Lundstrom, to whom I am indebted for knowledge of the document, which he has only recently found, as well as the Radford letter from which I quote several times, tells me that the Japanese report no aerial combat—difficult to understand since we had been heavily engaged at several times. But they do speak of seeing "more than three" night fighters turn on their lights. This had to have been the brief moment when our group, together for the only time that night, was illuminated, and it was at that point that, attracted by our lights, one of the Bettys, as confused and blinded as we were, tried to join up on the American formation. Looking to my right, I saw a long black cigar shape climb up from below and aft of Skon and swing into formation above us on our starboard side, behind and slightly above O'Hare. Realizing his fatal mistake, he began firing. "Butch, this is Phil. There's a Jap on your tail. Kernan, open fire." The intercom went dead as I began shooting back at the Betty, firing by our tail between Skon and O'Hare. The air was filled with gunfire. A long burst nearly emptied my ammunition can at the Betty to our rear, which, as the tracers arced toward him, broke away across our group to disappear in the darkness behind Skon.

Rand, in pain but staring hard out of the tunnel window, had a good view of the exchange of fire, but he missed O'Hare's plane slipping under us, just forward of Skon, and away in the dark. I thought I saw O'Hare reappear off to port, for the briefest glimpse, and then he was gone. Something whitish-gray appeared above the water, his parachute or the splash of the plane going in. Skon slid away instantly to follow O'Hare, and then returned to join up on us again when he could not find him.

Admiral Radford's letter of December 4 summarizes what happened. "Eventually the night fighter group was rendezvoused and established their identity by turning on their running lights. Shortly after this an enemy plane joined the formation on the starboard side. This plane and the fighter [O'Hare] flying on that side crossed over to port and then disappeared. This was the last seen of our fighter and subsequent careful search failed to locate the pilot." What happened to the Betty is not known, but it may be that it was the third plane the Japanese reported lost from the 752 Air Group that night—Phillips shot down only two—and Lundstrom speculates that it may have stumbled into the antiaircraft fire that flared up from time to time for the remainder of the night.

Phillips took us down to drag the surface for another long half-hour before giving up and making our way about 2100 back to the *Enterprise*. Skon landed first without any trouble. But for us the evening was by no means over. We still had to make a landing on an unlighted carrier deck at night. If it had been done before, it was certainly not standard procedure, and Phillips, despite having a thousand hours as an instrument instructor, had never done it, even in practice. We homed on the white wake that marked the ship in the water, but there was no light anywhere on deck except the fluorescent wands of the landing signal officer standing on the end of the flight deck. We came in too high, and just as Phillips was about to cut the engine the landing signal officer waved us off. Full throttle, nearly stalling out, wheels, flaps, and hook down, we hung for a moment above the deck, neither rising nor falling. In the bright blue light of the exhausts I saw the huge, dark shape of the carrier's island structure just a few feet off our starboard wing, the parked planes on the deck just a few feet below, the men standing there looking up at us. We hung there for an eternity, then picked up speed all at once and flew away to go around again.

The *Enterprise* captain, Matt Gardner, must have known we would never make it with the cumbersome plane in the dark, the pilot tensed to the snapping point, so he courageously turned on the shaded lights that marked out the flight deck for the crucial moment. They could only be seen from low and aft by a plane approaching for a landing, so they didn't reveal the ship very much for very long to a submarine or the Bettys still flying about.

This time it worked. We dropped heavily on the deck. The corpsmen took Rand away, Phillips disappeared to talk to the admiral, and I, still crouched on the turret seat, straightened out my legs with great pain and made my way to the head just below the flight deck, where I stood and pissed for what seemed like five minutes. Where did it all come from, on and on, emptying all the accumulated fear and tension out with the water that had built up in the longest three hours of my life, before or since.

Really messy firefights don't sort themselves out in the mind clearly, either sooner or later, and heavy feelings of responsibility and guilt lurk around all combat deaths. Without doubt I had fired at the trailing Japanese plane that tried to join up on us, and he had fired at everything in his range, including O'Hare and us, but had I, blasting away, hit the group commander as well? Like the cigar-shaped Betty sliding out of the darkness to our rear, guilt felt still for my mother's death slid across my mind. No one else on the flight had any doubts about what had happened, though we all saw the action from different angles. But my question would shortly be voiced openly in an unpleasant way by a newspaperman.

My first encounter with media arrogance came before I was even out of the head. He came charging in and while I was still standing at the urinal trough asked, "What happened? Where were they? How many? Where is O'Hare? How many did you shoot down?" The tone was hoarsely aggressive, and I discovered that I felt that the night flight was a complicated and deeply personal thing. I certainly didn't feel like talking about it to anyone as abrasive and unpleasant as this man. He bored right in, though, and began to try to construct the scandal he wanted. "How far away from O'Hare were you when he was hit? Were you shooting too?" And then, there it was: "Did you hit him?"

Letting me know that he was somehow an official who had a right to news and that anything of interest belonged to the public, especially his newspaper, he played on my doubts and shock to try to get some sudden, unconsidered remark that could be gotten by the censor and turned into sensational fare for his readers. If he had come at me with more sympathy I might have tried to tell him how mixed-up it all was, but his bullying got my back up, and I walked away shouting, "Get the hell away from me."

He went off muttering about reporting me to the officers, as if I had broken some kind of rule by not telling his newspaper all, but he never came back. I suppose the public relations officer—we had one by then—got hold of him, and in the end he wrote a number of stories for magazines like *The*

O'Hare Shot Down in the Pacific; Comrades Describe Night-Fight

By The Associated Press.

ABOARD A U. S. CARRIER IN THE CENTRAL PACIFIC, Nov. 29 (Delayed)—Lieut. Comdr. Edward H. (Butch) O'Hare, famous fighter pilot, was shot down in a night air battle over the central Pacific two nights ago while American airmen were breaking up an attack of thirty or forty Japanese torpedo planes on a United States carrier force, his flying companions said today.

Stories told by a squadron commander, a fighter pilot, radioman and gunner, the last to see O'Hare in the air, were not in complete agreement. But the action was swift and in the darkness, with the blinding of tracer fire and the flames from burning planes as the main illumination, so it was natural that none of them would know exactly what happened.

"For three days Butch and I were standing by for our Japanese-stalking attack," said Lieut. Comdr. John L. Phillips Jr., 33 years old, of Linden, Va. "Butch was the first off the deck. We had difficulty sticking together when it got dark. But we were lucky and were joining up when we ran smack into the Japs rendezvousing.

"Butch came up on my starboard and Wingman Skon on the port. Then my gunner Kernan saw a fourth plane coming up below Butch. I gave him permission to fire as soon as we were within range. At the same time I overhauled a Jap and got into his slipstream and at fifty yards knocked him into a tea kettle.

"Meanwhile, on the other side of our carrier task force, thirty miles distant, a Jap dropped a series of flares for a torpedo attack illumination and our ships were clearly outlined.

"I was closing in on a second Jap when the fireworks started. I was shooting at a Jap, and my gunner was shooting at a Jap who in turn was shooting at O'Hare.

"My target exploded and blew up beautifully, with at least a quarter of a mile torch of gasoline trailing behind him before he hit the water.

"While I was watching the Jap burn I saw something drop straight off into the water, making a big splash. Then I thought, 'My God, that may be Butch.'

"I attempted to make contact, calling, 'Butch, this is Phil' over and over, but I got no response. I kept thinking that the splash lasted a long time and that it may have been Butch's parachute. Now I think it was a Jap plane which Butch shot down."

Ensign Warren A. Skon, 24, of St. Paul, Minn., who was flying wing on O'Hare when they started to join Phillips, said "the air was suddenly thick with Japs.

"One Jap had dropped a flare and this may have been the plane Phillips shot down.

"As we joined on Commander Phillips, Butch said: 'You take the side you want!' I said, 'I'll take the port.'

"'Roger,' he said, and that was the last word he said.

"Then I saw tracers around his plane. I saw it sheer off and drop quickly below us."

Among Last to See Him

Another version of the last seen of O'Hare, termed by President Roosevelt one of the greatest combat fliers of all time, was told by Aviation Ordnance Man Alvin B. Kernan, 20, of Saratoga, Wyo., who was among the last to see the commander.

"I saw Butch and Skon joining up," he said. "Then as I looked to the starboard, a fourth plane was closing in on us. It was very dark, but because I could see Skon off our port I knew this was a Jap.

"I informed Mr. Phillips and he gave me permission to fire as soon as he was in range. My tracer fire seemed to go into him, but I was blinded by tracers and my gun muzzle, which was white with heat. I don't know whether I shot down the Jap.

"While I was firing I saw Commander O'Hare do a wingover across the top of us and he disappeared into the darkness. A few

Lieut. Comdr. Edward H. O'Hare
Associated Press Wirephoto

of Chapel Hill, Va. His searching planes carried red dye markers and float lights and in their bomb bays a waterproof bag containing a radio kit and a shipwreck kit with food, water, cigarettes, fishing gear and blankets.

The reconstructed story of the men who flew with O'Hare indicated that the lieutenant commander took one Japanese torpedo plane down with him. It was his ninth.

But forever it will be remembered how Butch saved our task force from the heaviest and longest Japanese torpedo plane night attack.

Greatest Feat Recalled

Commenting on that action, Rear Admiral Arthur W. Radford, commander of the task force, said:

"Butch, with accompanying planes, saved my formation from certain torpedo hits. I am recommending him for a second Congressional Medal of Honor."

An aviator who knew him said: "Despite our great engines of destruction, enormous tanks, guns of battleships and carriers—it remains that one determined man can settle a battle."

Butch O'Hare's aide, Lieut. Wallace M. Parker of Pittsburgh, Pa., added: "Butch did it twice."

Commander O'Hare received a Congressional Medal of Honor for shooting down five Japanese planes, single handed, which attempted to attack the aircraft carrier Lexington in the South Seas in 1942.

moments later it seemed that he reappeared and made an outside loop. Then he was gone."

Lieut. (J. G.) Hazen B. Rand, 25, of Avon, Mass., who was shot through the foot during the action, said:

"I saw a fourth plane's guns blinking red and he was shooting at Butch while our gunner, Kernan, was shooting at the Jap.

"I overheard Kernan tell Commander Phillips that he was opening fire and Phil in turn told Butch, 'Butch, there's a Jap plane coming into your tail.'

"Then Butch's lights went off. I looked again and he was gone."

Relentless Search Conducted

Commander O'Hare landed at Tarawa, for the first carrier plane landing there since the American conquest of the Gilbert Islands, to study the field. He also had a personal interest because he had "hellcatted" that area before and during the landing operations at Makin and Tarawa.

Since dawn of Nov. 27 a relentless search for him has been conducted by carrier groups and by planes from Tarawa. The search allows for a twenty-mile drift due to the heavy Gilbert currents. An area of 2,000 square miles has been criss-crossed, boxed and scouted.

Oil slicks and jetsam from enemy planes and a blue-gray overturned Japanese liferaft were found by Acting Torpedo Plane Squadron Commander Bill Privette

The New York Times report of the nightfighter action, the first in naval history, in which O'Hare was killed off the Gilbert Islands on November 27, 1943.

Saturday Evening Post, describing O'Hare going down amid a blaze of enemy gunfire while saving a grateful fleet, with bouquets to everyone else involved, including me. The official publicized navy version was not so garish, but it downplayed the separation of the fighter planes and the torpedo plane, bringing them together much earlier than they had in fact joined up and crediting the entire group with two certain, and two possible, kills. The *Enterprise's* Action Report claimed only two. The separation of the fighters and the torpedo plane from the beginning of the fight was obviously a major defect in the operation, and in his report of December 4, Admiral Radford explicitly expressed his displeasure. "The two fighters were launched first, and, contrary to instructions issued by Commander Task Group 50.2 [Radford] and without his knowledge, the fighters were vectored out to intercept the enemy planes without having rendezvoused with the TBF."

The intelligence officer gave me a cup of his famous coffee and debriefed me, and then I sat on the deck in a corner of the ready room for a long time talking to a few friends, Boone and Varner mostly, trying to sort the whole thing out. I tried to sleep, but the cold from the air conditioning—usually thought a luxury—in the old converted ready room that was our crew compartment began to make me imagine that I was dead. Everyone else was comfortable, snoring away, so it was in my head, but it didn't go away for a time. Shivering, I went over the fight again and again, trying to sort it out and only tangling it up more. I began to brood about my bad luck, having had the orders to flight school that would have sent me back to the States rather than sitting here waiting to get killed, if not tonight then tomorrow, when we would be sure to go up again, having had so much success tonight.

O'Hare was a great loss to the navy, but there was little sentimentality expressed openly for his death. Partly this was professional sangfroid, partly it was that between officers and enlisted men an impermeable filter blocked all transmission of emotion. Phillips was quite buoyed up by being credited with two enemy planes, unheard of for a torpedo pilot. O'Hare was recommended for another Congressional Medal of Honor, but in the end everyone on the flight received the Navy Cross, which surprised me, for I thought that being the only enlisted man involved I would be left out or given a token. But I was treated as quite the hero. Phillips became the group commander.

We sat and waited again on the next two nights, and once we got up to the deck and into the planes. But at the last minute the radar contact faded and the flight was called off. By the next night we were gone—Tarawa and

Makin having been secured—on our way at high speed for the Marshall Islands, from where the Bettys had come, with a view of knocking out the airfields and shipping in preparation for the invasion that would come the next month. Death never went very far away, and on November 30 one of our planes loaded with depth charges on antisubmarine patrol crashed in the water alongside the ship. While we watched the crew swimming in the water, the depth charges exploded.

The morning of the attack, December 4, 1943, was cool, the sun just rising as we sat on the hangar deck with the breeze blowing through the open curtains. I stood by the plane looking at the sun, wondering how I had gotten to that particular place when so many other Americans who had more at stake were not there. Dark thoughts soon passed and fate was accepted in the excitement of taking off and taking the lead of the entire air group on the way to the target. From twenty thousand feet the whole atoll, which would soon be taken by American troops, spread out before us in an enormous circle of narrow white-beached islands, with a deep blue lagoon in the center. The morning was beautiful and clear, visibility unlimited. In the lagoon several Japanese cruisers, unprepared, were getting under way. Black antiaircraft bursts rocked the plane, and the fighter planes taking off from Roi-Namur far below seemed more interesting than ominous. A Japanese float plane going the other way flew by us, but I only recognized it after it had passed, and there was no point in firing.

As our bombers attacked the cruisers and the fighters strafed the Japanese planes on the ground, Air Group 6 proceeded in a lordly way, southward across the lagoon to the largest island, Kwajalein, at the southern tip, to attack the ground installations and the shipping in the anchorage. We circled and watched, calling attention to targets, and as the last planes finished their runs and left, we went in alone to bomb a merchant ship. We pushed over in a steep dive from twenty thousand feet, and as we neared the bottom of our run through the thick antiaircraft fire, Phillips began firing his guns, which seemed rather pointless. As we pulled up and I thought gratefully, "Now I can go to San Francisco," Phillips came on the intercom and admitted wryly that in the dive he had made the mistake of pressing the gun trigger on the front of the stick rather than the bomb release on the top of the stick. Too bad, I thought, but let's get the hell out of here and get me off to flight school. The thought never occurred to him, and around we went for another run, with everything in the area shooting at us. The bombs seemed to hit the ship, but the painfully learned fact is that it is always impossible to tell for certain, even with photographs, and those who make the bomb runs are understandably optimistic about results.

The return to Pearl Harbor went quietly, and even before the ship anchored I said goodbye to everyone and flew with Phillips and Sullivan for the last time to Pearl Harbor, and from there I went by boat to Ewa, the marine field where people going to flight training out of the fleet were assembled. Most of the squadron I never saw again. O'Hare's memory was honored by naming the largest airport in the United States O'Hare Field, in Chicago. Phillips was killed a few months later at Truk. As air group commander he was shifted from a torpedo plane to a fighter. No one saw what happened, and the plane was never found in the Truk lagoon, where there was every kind of wreckage imaginable, but the theory was that flying over the battle and directing the attack on the Japanese Pearl Harbor, a Japanese fighter came in on him from the rear. Accustomed to flying in a plane where the gunner kept an eye out on that part of the sky, Phillips was probably so completely absorbed in directing the attack, he never knew what hit him.

TEN

Drifting

One of the advantages the United States had over the Japanese was the ability to replace its losses, including its skilled manpower. At the beginning of the war, the Japanese had trained a superior group of naval aviators, but so lengthy and so thorough was the process that they never undertook training a second cadre. It was as if they thought the first group so good that they could never die. But the first group died with incredible bravery in one battle after another, and their places were then taken by recruits with only a few hours of training time and no battle experience. The U.S. Navy, however, put a pilot-training program into place before the war and kept running it to produce a steady stream of replacements. By 1943 heavy casualties were expected and the number of trainees had been increased sharply. Enlisted men from the fleet were allowed to compete, and it was as a member of this group that I got my chance to be a pilot and an officer at the beginning of 1944. I was still romantic enough to find the idea exciting, and it seemed to me that I was on the verge of great things.

From Pearl Harbor in early December I went back by ship to San Diego, where I was given a train ticket to San Francisco and told to report to naval headquarters and be assigned to flight training. I stopped to see the Boones, who were, as always, most hospitable. The oldest son of the family, Bill, was an operator who had contacts with everyone, including Frank Sinatra, who was just then extremely popular. Bill took me to one of Sinatra's radio programs and introduced us. Sinatra was extremely pleasant, and later we went to his house and a party that never seemed to close down. I never talked to Sinatra again, but the drinks were free and the girls rather remarkable. Someone asked me if I had any gas coupons, gas being rationed and in short supply at that time. When I said, "No," they produced a big wad, all counterfeit or stolen, I suppose, but I took them gratefully and used them to drive around while on leave.

Bill Boone also knew people on the newspaper and arranged for pictures and interviews with me about the death of Butch O'Hare. I was doubtful about this kind of publicity, and it must have showed since the article, when it was published, called me "modest little Alvin Kernan." After I was in flight training Dick Boone, to my chagrin and the laughter of the other cadets, sent me a letter addressed to "Modest Alvin Kernan."

It was near Christmas when I got to San Francisco, and I expected to get some kind of leave, but since I had had thirty days' leave the previous March, I had used up my quota for that year and was ordered to report to Flight Training School at San Luis Obispo, in the old California Polytechnic Institute. Complaints about it being Christmas, about having missed out on leave in 1942, *and* a quart of good whiskey the Boones had given me persuaded the yeoman to delay my assignment to the next class, thus automatically giving me a thirty-day leave. Nothing could have seemed better, and I took up residence in the elegant Claremont Hotel on the ridge overlooking the bay in Oakland. In a few days I had just enough money left to buy a ticket to Saratoga.

It was bitterly cold and, having feted me only nine months earlier, the people seemed rather disappointed to see me home again so soon. In the meantime, the comings and goings of servicemen, many of whom had been in combat, were getting commonplace. The girls had all gotten married or had gone out to work in the California aircraft factories, and besides, I was flat broke. Frank Kernan, my stepfather, had managed to get elected justice of the peace, which meant that he could fine, and keep part of the fines, speeders and hunters and fishermen who were caught with too many deer or fish. He ran a small store in Saratoga, sold insurance, repaired electrical appliances, and kept a line of small gifts and greeting cards. It looked like the apothecary's shop in *Romeo and Juliet*, but it kept, just barely, with the aid of my allotment, a roof over his head and food on the table. I slept on a spare bed in the back of the store and drove around the county on icy roads with my illegal gas coupons looking up old friends and making dates with girls in Medicine Bow and Rawlins who had different goals in life than I did at that point.

In the end I was glad to go back to California, knowing that somehow I had left Wyoming for good and that I would never go back to stay. Los Angeles was warm and lively for a few days, but by the time I got to San Luis

Back in the States in December 1943 with a group of other sailors from the fleet being sent to flight training.

Obispo in late January, the winter rains had set in and life got difficult. Flight Prep School was designed mostly as a way of toughening up the V-5 cadets physically and was run by a bunch of old coaches from high schools and colleges who delighted in putting us through endless exercises, obstacle courses, endurance swims, long-distance runs, speed-agility exercises, and so on. The marines among us, many of them yellow from the Atabrine they took to prevent malaria, were tough, but most of the sailors were soft, and many of us were clumsy in the way country boys are who have gone to schools where there were no sports programs.

Learning how to leap over walls, climb ropes, swing on trapezes, and so on came hard and painfully, but we were young and keen. Better here, it seemed, than back in the Pacific where the great drive across the center of the ocean to Japan was rolling in earnest now. The other training—aeronautics, meteorology, Morse code, navigation—was easy for me, though I got so cocky that I failed a major navigational test, carelessly taking the original heading in exactly the opposite direction—180 degrees off—and having to attend remedial classes for a time.

Mostly it rained, and we lined up outside our grim barracks at six in the morning, standing in the pouring rain day after day. We worked, stood guard, ran to class, exercised, and ate soaking wet. Colds were endemic. It was a dull and depressing life without any recreation. Midway through the three-month course we were given a thirty-six-hour liberty, from noon on Saturday to midnight on Sunday. San Luis Obispo is about equidistant from Los Angeles and San Francisco, which meant about two hundred miles either way.

The entire coast was loaded with camps, and there must have been literally millions of soldiers, sailors, and marines in that area, all of them trying on a weekend to get on the few buses and trains. The bus depot where I went to catch a ride to Los Angeles looked like the hold of an immigrant ship, and I would never have gotten on the bus except for a friend, a former marine sergeant named Joey Bishop. An Oklahoma Indian, he was short, dark, wiry, and a Guadalcanal veteran. I coached him in some of the subjects and in return he helped me get through some of the more difficult parts of the training, like hand-to-hand combat and all-out wrestling, at which he excelled and I did not. He instantly saw that getting aboard the bus in the normal way was hopeless, and without hesitating, he went up the high side of the bus and into one of the windows, holding out a hand to help me up and through. It was dark by the time we got to Los Angeles, and we immediately headed for the bars. By noon the next day it was time to try to board another bus to take our dreadful hangovers back to San Luis Obispo. We got there by midnight, cold and exhausted, and I then stood watch from midnight to 0400, trying desperately to stay awake, while the rain never stopped dropping off the eaves.

At the end of the three-month course, there was to be a ball for the graduating class. With travel and accommodations what they were, it all seemed pretty hopeless, but girls came from all over the country to go to dinner in the mess hall, dance in the local hotel and stay there with chaperones, and walk the next day on Pismo Beach, famous for its clams. No matter what the circumstances, the war was the most exciting show in town, worth any amount of inconvenience. I persuaded Betty Boone to come up for the occasion. Her mother came along, to Betty's chagrin, to make sure that she was safe among the soldiery and paid for it by spending the night in her hotel listening to servicemen shout obscenities in the street below as they hurled bottles at the wall of the hotel. We all walked up and down Pismo Beach the next day, not knowing what to say, and in the afternoon the Boones departed, gratefully, for Los Angeles.

Flight Training School was the next step, and we all went off the next day to various desolate little flying fields in the northwest to learn to fly, first Piper Cubs, and then the open-cockpit yellow biplanes, N2Ss. I drew a school run by a tiny Portland college, Lewis and Clark, out in the desert on the eastern border of Oregon, in a small town called Ontario, near the Snake River. We rode for days on some new kind of short boxcar that had been fitted up with shipboard-type bunks to transport troops, standing at the open door like hoboes looking out at the countryside. Lewis and Clark, with few students during the war, was keeping alive by running this program and had transformed an old barn into a dormitory, mess hall, and classroom, next to a small macadamized flying field with one modest hangar.

We were all wild to learn to fly, but there was still physical training, a fiendish obstacle course that we learned to cheat by running with our heads turned watching the coach. When he looked away we dived through the lower rungs of contraptions we were supposed to climb and ran around walls. He knew we were a bunch of slackers and so put great store in the "step test" as a scientific way of measuring our lack of fitness. In the test you stepped up on a bench knee-high in front of you, and then stepped down, 120 counts to the minute, for five minutes. Sounds easy, but it was incredibly tiring. At the end our pulse was measured and fitness was determined by the speed with which you returned to normal. I had low blood pressure to begin with, so my heart rate didn't have far to go to get back to normal, and on the chart I always registered as extremely fit. Since the coach had me down as a goof-off and a miserable athlete, my scores infuriated him, but he seems never to have thought of determining whether we all began with the same pulse rate. His faith in the uniformity of nature was as absolute as it was unwarranted.

The town of Ontario was a pleasant little place to which we were allowed to go frequently and without supervision, there being almost no discipline in the barracks. Liquor was rationed and sold only in state stores, but you could keep your weekly bottle in a locker club where, when you asked for a drink, you would give the bartender a key and he would solemnly open a wooden locker where your whiskey was stored. For only a modest service charge he would pour out a shot, return the bottle to the locker, give you back the key, and provide ice and whatever else was needed. It all had a satisfactory, cere-monial quality to it; offering a friend a drink was a meaningful ritual, and life was generally agreeable.

But it was flying that we were here for, and after a couple of weeks we at last got into the cabin of the little Piper Cubs, with the instructor sitting in back, and took off into the high pale sunny Oregon sky. After flying for years in warplanes, the light plane with its washing-machine engine seemed a bit risky, but it moved around with agility and it was assuringly safe, getting out of spins easily and gliding for miles without power. Turns, climbs, dives, spins, stalls, slips, the third dimension of space opened up endless new possibilities of movement, and we practiced for two hours every day, six days a week, whenever we were not running the obstacle course or studying more navigation and meteorology. You were supposed to solo after between six and ten hours of instruction, and most of us did. Takeoffs and landings were the trickiest part, mostly because of the usual strong cross winds on the one runway. This meant that you couldn't land straight on but had to come in to one side and high and then slip down and across to the end of the runway, just a few feet above ground, pull level, and stall the plane out into a nice smooth landing. Usually there was a heavy bump, and the plane would bounce back into the air and come down with another crash. Too many of these heavy landings ruined planes and washed you out, as did ground loops that came from getting caught in the cross wind or applying too much of the wrong brake while rolling down the field.

As soon as we learned to fly the Cubs we were clamoring to get into the Yellow Perils, and we did after a month. This was different: more power, an open cockpit, a lot of response on the controls. After a few hours of instruction in these biplanes we began to fly them for two hours each day, each plane being sent out to a separate sector somewhere above the Oregon desert, keeping track of your position by watching the Snake River, practicing one maneuver after another.

On our own with airplanes we became adventurous, and there were games like flying under bridges—recklessly dangerous considering how inexperienced we were as pilots. Then there was the trick of getting above and behind a farmer plowing, throttling back, then slipping quietly down until just above him, and suddenly cutting in the engine full power and diving directly down over the horses or tractor. The farmers came to loathe us, quite justly, and called in regularly to report us, but somehow we survived. The worst, and therefore the most delightful, stunt was to find a stretch of straight highway, of which there were many out in the desert, and fly along it with the wheels just off the ground. The trick here was to catch a car coming from the opposite direction and fly straight at him until just before hitting, when you came back on the stick and jumped over the terrified driver.

We were real menaces to the life and limbs of others as well as ourselves, and only in wartime would the countryside have put up with us.

Just before we left my medal came through. Twenty-five or thirty cadets lined up to hear the station commander read the citation and pin the Navy Cross on me. I kept the medal on, the only time in my life I ever wore it, while we all went inside and ate the cinnamon buns for which the cook was famous. Then I put it in its box to keep and pass on to my children. It all seemed too domestic, sitting there munching warm buns, in contrast to the wild night for which the medal was awarded. The Navy Cross carried with it a monthly payment of three dollars, which in time I duly got and drew for the remainder of my time in the navy.

The casualties the navy had expected had not materialized, and by now there were far too many pilots in training. One way of handling the problem was leave, and we were, at the end of our three months in Ontario, sent off for fifteen days. I thought that with my new cadet's uniform, though without any stripes, I would cut quite a swathe in Saratoga. But by now they had all seen too much of me and other servicemen. Besides, they had grown blasé about the war. I hung around for a few days without much to do and then headed out to Los Angeles to see the Boones. Then I went up to Santa Rosa, where the old squadron, Torpedo Six, was back re-forming. Life in the squadron seemed much more interesting and exciting than life as an aviation cadet, especially since we did so little flying.

The other thing the navy could do to slow down the already long time of pilots' training was to add more steps. Having been to flight prep and flight training, I now went to preflight school at St. Mary's College, just back of Oakland, where we studied more navigation, did endless physical training, stayed hours in the pool. I learned to swim four different strokes and to stay afloat in the pool for six hours with my clothes on, but I got no closer to flying. Like many naval stations by the summer of '44, St. Mary's fielded numerous athletic teams, largely made up of professional athletes who had been drafted and were kept around simply to play various games. The football team at St. Mary's was a particularly rough bunch who unfortunately needed someone to practice against. We were issued football uniforms and sent out to provide them with raw meat. We never got the ball; we only lined up for them to block and to run over. But we weren't having any of it. The coaches exhorted us to stand up like men and threatened us with extra drill, but each time the center gave the ball to the quarterback on the professional team, we all instantly dropped where we were and covered up our heads with our arms. The backs got some pleasure I suppose out of running over us, but we kept our teeth intact and avoided broken bones.

About this time the navy admitted for the first time that they had too many pilots in training and that we could expect at the best about another year of training before we would get our wings. To many it seemed fine. Some risk in training accidents, but better than going out to the fleet again when the war was really heating up. I was still too romantic, though. V-5 was a dog's life, no freedom at all, constant running here and there being shouted at by a bunch of officers who had never been to sea, studying the same subjects over and over. I think in truth, though I didn't tell myself so at the time, that I found the cadet's life dull. I would rather take my chances, get my rating of first-class ordnanceman back, and live a little more exciting life. Of course, you always get more than you bargain for, and I did not anticipate then how exciting life would shortly become.

So I signed my resignation from V-5 and got in return a little paper thanking me for my patriotism and a ticket to Chicago and the Great Lakes Naval Training Station, where all the old cadets went to be reassigned. Those of us who had resigned and had been enlisted before flight training were lucky since we simply got our ratings back and were assigned to new duty. The cadets who had joined up from civilian life, however, along with those who washed out, had to go to boot camp and start everything from the beginning. Great Lakes for me was a huge wooden hangar filled with double-decker bunks and nothing else. Our old uniforms were sent to us from home, and we sat around day after day with nothing to do. Even cardplaying was out since we had no money, our pay records being lost, and to sailors, games without gambling are like food without salt.

There was one diversion—going to parties at night. The people of that area were almost mad with hospitality. A serviceman couldn't walk down the street without someone trying to get him to go home for a meal, join in a family party, stay the night. Milwaukee was most famous for this kind of generosity, and whenever you wanted a party you took the Skokie Valley Express, a terrifying train of trolley cars that rattled at seventy miles an hour from Chicago up to Milwaukee. As you came out of the train people were waiting on the platform to round servicemen up for some kind of a party or another. Since then, as now, there was entertainment and there was entertainment, the trick was to spot and join quickly some group of patriots, preferably represented by pretty girls, that looked like drinking and dancing were part of the fun, rather than praying and hymn singing.

If your constitution was especially robust that day you went with one of the many Polish groups. Strong young men holding beer kegs overhead while everyone filled their mugs, faces red with the effort and hernias threatening to explode. Endless polkas going faster and faster. My mind still responds to a beer-sodden stomping out of the "Beer Barrel Polka"—"Roll out the barrel, we'll have a barrel of fun"—louder and louder, faster and faster. The girls, all of whom had reverted to their native Polish costumes, were beautiful and devoted to nothing but dancing, faster and faster, no pause for anything else. Finally, exhausted and boozy, you were taken back to the Skokie Valley Express in the early hours of the morning to rattle—every rattle inside the head as well as in the wheels—back to Chicago and the gloom of the barracks. Still, after being entertained in Milwaukee in the aerie of some brood of Polish Falcons, you were glad to sit around and breathe quietly for a day or two.

There were almost no restrictions on us, and, always broke, after a few days of hanging around, I went to Chicago and got a daytime job working in the package section of the post office, unloading the mail cars and distributing the packages to various chutes that took them to other cars headed for other places. It was bitterly cold in the shed and the heavy mailbags were hard on the hands, but we were paid at the end of each day and could go out to the bars to drink and look for girls.

After a time I got another hourly job in a small defense plant in an old factory, loading huge iron bars of three or four hundred pounds' weight on a tottering dolly and moving them onto an elevator and up to another floor where they were dumped in another pile on the ground. I never knew what happened to them or what the plant made, but at 5:00 P.M. each day the paymaster would give us cash for whatever hours we had worked. It was brutal work and I was exhausted after eight hours. By then I had moved into town and taken a room at a hotel that demanded payment daily, there being a great shortage of rooms. After I bought a meal and paid the daily rent there was nothing left over, and so the next day I would go to the factory again and wrestle with those huge bars until it was time to eat and fall into bed exhausted. I stuck with this routine for about a week, calling in each day to be sure that no orders had come for me to report to duty someplace. Then the pointlessness of it began to seep in.

I went back to the training station and wangled a week's leave, which they were glad to give me since no one knew what to do with the flood of sailors who were coming in from pilot training. I was by no means the only one who had opted for the enlisted ranks again. A Red Cross worker offered me a train ticket home, but when I tried to get cash rather than the ticket, knowing that there was no point in going back to Wyoming again, she sensed that I was trying to work a deal and withdrew the offer. I decided to let chance decide about where to spend the leave, went to the Greyhound bus depot, and asked how far twelve dollars and something, almost all my accumulated savings from work, would take me. It would, it turned out, take me quite a distance, to Bemidji, Minnesota, one of the record cold spots in the country, right up on the Canadian border. I used a bit more money to wire Bernice, a schoolteacher whom I had met in Saratoga in the spring of '42, and she agreed to meet me in Minneapolis and pay for the room and a meal or two. It was most generous of her. She was about to set out for a new job teaching in Salem, Oregon, and had little enough herself, having worked as a cashier in a restaurant for the last year. Looking back, I took advantage of her, for she cared more for me by a lot than I for her, but perhaps she too looked forward to an exciting change from her routine.

The meeting was not a success. We were both too tense. She wanting marriage, even knowing that I was surely one of the last candidates in the world for marriage. So I put her on the bus for Salem in tears and anger and took another bus north. The Lord did provide, for I soon got to talking to a sailor going home on leave to Bemidji. He was a reader, as I was, and we talked happily of books, John Dos Passos's USA was a favorite of mine then, but for the most part I read at random, not knowing who or what to read. Curt had been to a year of college and told me about Thomas Wolfe and other books. Asked where I was going, I replied that I had a ticket to Bemidji and hoped to find a place to stay when I got there. He at once invited me to stay at his house, and I did for a couple of days, talking and going fishing for pickerel with him in the nearby lake. His leave was short and he was off soon. After the war I was driving through Chicago and tried to call Curt to see if he had made it. He had not, but died in an unusual way. Stabbed, his mother said, by a lunatic who came up to him on a Chicago street and put a knife in his heart. Mistaken identity, fury, no one knew.

Two girls who worked for the local dentist arranged for me to stay with the family of one, where I was fed, questioned, and treated like a hero. During the day I would hang around the dental office—the dentist never seemed to be there, and I often wondered where *he* spent his time—sitting in the chair and flirting with the girls. They would clean my teeth from time to time, treat my gums, and provide other dental services. An odd kind of an idyll, but I remember it as having a peculiar dental luxuriance associated strangely with the mouth and the teeth. In a day or so it was time to go back, but I had been broke for some time. The local USO, however, provided a rail ticket back to Chicago. For many the memory of World War II must be sitting up, desperately tired, trying to find some way to sleep in a rattling railroad day coach, with constant movement up and down the aisle, drafts, lights, shifting this way and that, trying to find some way of stretching out, the smell of old green dusty plush seats. Another of those nights and I was back in Chicago, stiff, exhausted, hoping to God there would at last be orders sending me to some kind of regular duty.

There were. I had hoped that after two tours of overseas duty I would get to stay stateside for a while. But the orders were for Torpedo Squadron Forty, a squadron that had been formed in 1943 and been land based on Guadalcanal from late '43 into '44 to attack the Japanese in the Solomons and Rabaul. Now they had been joined with a fighter squadron to form a small air group, number 40, which was to go on a medium-sized escort carrier, converted from a tanker, the USS *Suwanee* (CVE 27), an awkward, slow, unattractive old waddler that had been on more invasions than any other navy ship, from North Africa to the Philippines, where her flight deck had been blown off on the day the Japanese fleet broke through to take the support ships under fire.

I was soon off to Los Alamitos, California, a navy field just to the northeast of Long Beach, where VT-40 was in training. Another long train ride back to the California sunshine, but when I got to Los Alamitos in early November, the squadron had transferred to Livermore, about twenty miles to the east of San Francisco Bay. I was given a ticket and sent on my way once more, but I couldn't pass up a chance to see the Boones again, and their hospitality was so warm that I decided to spend a full day sitting around with them. When I did arrive at Livermore I assumed that no one would note the missing day in all the confusion of transfer, but the personnel officer did. He was a relentless character, and he used to pop up from time to time, hoping to catch me off guard, I think, and ask me why I had been a day late in reporting. I had no acceptably good answer, so all I could say was that I had come along as fast as I could, missed trains, and some other mumblings, all as indistinct as possible. These responses seemed, to my surprise, to infuriate him, and it was months before he gave up pursuing me.

Livermore in November and December was foggy and cold, with no heat in the barracks. We sat around in light clothing shivering, waiting for the fog to clear so that training flights could go up, but most days we were grounded. Although I was an aerial gunner, there was no opening for me. I was not sorry, in all that fog, and happily worked in the ordnance ground crew loading practice bombs, cleaning machine guns, synchronizing bomb racks, and frequently cleaning the officers' pistols. They all believed in going out heavily armed, and they liked their pistols broken down and cleaned often. Sometimes for a little money we cut and put clear plastic grips on the guns for them, often with a picture of their wife or girl underneath. These little ways of earning money had a Chinese name, "cumshaw."

I found a few friends, no one I had known before, and one of the few real friends I made in the navy, Jim Loughridge, from near Buffalo, who shared my interest in books. He introduced me to *Ulysses* and we went into San Francisco to the opera, or at least the operetta *Student Prince,* and to bars to talk about books like Arthur Koestler's *Darkness at Noon.* He was a rather dapper young man with ideas well in advance of mine about living well, and together we searched out good restaurants and on New Year's Eve, for the first time in my life, drank champagne, horrible wartime champagne, but festive nonetheless.

Bernice came down from Salem, Oregon, by bus, but again it was an awkward meeting. After a short stay she went back to Oregon, depressed. Loughridge came down sick and was sent off to a hospital. He had been flying with the commanding officer, Lieutenant Campbell, and I now took over his turret for a few flights. Campbell was as dour as his name, and we didn't get along very well, so soon parted. But at least flying with the captain got the personnel officer to stop asking me about the missing day.

Cigarettes were now in short supply everywhere, and Mrs. Boone, who smoked like a chimney, as they used to say, was suffering from nicotine privation. She asked me to send cigarettes, any cigarettes I could find, and I did. We were rationed at the ship's store, and since I smoked heavily myself, I used up what I could buy that way. There were, however, numerous cigarette machines about the base, and armed with all the change I could find, I went about getting some of the strangest brand names I ever saw and mailing off care packages to Mrs. Boone. Knowing what we know now about smoking, it seems almost criminal that the services supported smoking the way they did. Cigarettes aboard ship throughout the war were five cents a pack, and since we sat about so much of the time, smoking was for almost everyone a major occupation. But no one knew at the time the connection between various

Back at sea again in February 1945 on board the USS *Suwanee*, an escort carrier, with a new pilot, Ensign Bob Dyer, and Radioman "Moon" Mullins.

diseases and smoking, and smoking was considered rather manly, so we all puffed away, and paid the price, as I did, many years later.

It was never bitterly cold in Livermore but always foggy and damp, and everyone tried as much as possible to get away for liberty to San Francisco, San Jose, or some other warmer place. I began flying again with one or another of the new ensigns who made up most of the squadron and ended up with the youngest of them all, Bob Dyer, known as "Irish," from Illinois, and his radioman, Oscar Mullins, a Georgia boy with a dish face, inevitably called "Moon" after the old comic-strip character Moon Mullins.

I was a veteran by now and felt a bit superior to this small air group, destined for a small converted carrier doing some kind of dull escort duty. Most of the pilots and aircrewmen were new to their jobs and seemed naive about the war and the service, meaning they were still enthusiastic and expected great things to happen. The old-timers like myself, aged twenty, knew that whatever was going to happen would be tedious and anticlimactic. But the little ship we were destined for was headed for some big-time action.

In early February orders came to move the planes and the crew to the Alameda Naval Air Station, just to the east of where the Bay Bridge comes into Oakland. For a few days we were in barracks there, given liberty in San Francisco every night. We were all absolutely broke, as usual, but we went on liberty anyway, on the theory that any liberty is better than life aboard ship and that we had better store up as much of it as possible for the future. We went and stared at the Mark Hopkins Hotel, about which a wildly popular novel, *Shore Leave* by Frederic Wakeman, had been written. Wakeman told the story of a group of pilots returning from the Pacific after a long cruise and taking rooms in the *Mark*, where they got fabulously drunk and reeled from one beautiful girl to another.

It was all a dream, though a warming one, but the fate of most of us was to go down to the USO and drink free coffee, hoping to get a chance to dance with one of the few weary girls who were grimly doing their part in the war by being friendly to the servicemen. They were nice girls, I thought, but inevitably they ended up having to dance with the most unwashed soldiers and sailors, wrestling with them courageously and crying out for help only when distressed, as they often were. The girls looked stricken when the shore patrol hauled the culprits off, usually after banging them on the head with a club for a bit, feeling somehow responsible for the lust they had aroused, however innocently. I had always thought that men had it a lot harder in this life than women, but I learned a lot in that USO about how hard it is for young women, and some not so young, to deal with a situation they cannot escape.

Sailors everywhere and at all times know that no matter how hard sea duty is, there is always a relief in going aboard ship and leaving land behind. So it was that on February 8, 1945, we picked up our gear and went aboard the USS *Suwanee*, lying at the Alameda dock. The planes were hoisted aboard, and we were ready to sail.

ELEVEN

War's End

Two of the old hands from Torpedo Forty were still missing as the gangways began to come up, but then the broken-down car they had bought came roaring down to the dock, pulling right up to the edge at high speed and screeching to a stop. Both sailors jumped out, running for the last gangway, and then one turned back, opened the driver's door, released the brake, and gave the car a push off the end of the dock into San Francisco Bay. The crew stood on the deck cheering wildly as Cletus Powell leaped several feet of water to land on the quarterdeck and ask the officer-of-the-deck for permission to come aboard. It was a gallant gesture, but Powell should have missed the ship.

Leaving San Francisco Bay, sailing under the Golden Gate Bridge, picking up the long Pacific swells, and looking back on the white cities on the hills was one of the great scenes of the Pacific war. It was powerful not only in retrospect, as so many events are after the future is known, but at the moment it took place. Everyone went to quarters in undress blue uniforms, lining the flight deck as we went under the bridge, and the ship's horn sounded a salute to the country left behind and got in return blasts from all the other ships in the harbor. It was valedictory, a moving, powerful sensory image of a country united in war. Every man must have wondered whether he would ever come back again—I know I did—and wondered too how many of those standing with him would return. It was sentimental but it was real. My eyes moved from one face to another of men who are as alive to me now as they ever were but whose bones are washing around the bottom of the sea, tangled in the wreckage of their planes, between Okinawa and Taiwan, near islands with such romantic names as Ishigaki, Miyako, and Kerama-rettō.

By February 16 we were at Pearl Harbor, but a week later we were at sea again, crossing the International Date Line on February 28 and the equator on March 2.

The day before that crossing we crashed on a catapult launch. The catapult was a long open rail running about fifty feet to the forward edge of the flight deck, with a trolley that ran inside the rail. A plane was positioned at the rear of the catapult rail, and the trolley was attached to its wheels by two cables leading up to hooks on the inside wheel struts. At the rear the plane was anchored by a hook attached to the deck by means of a tension ring just strong enough to hold the plane in place when it was turned up to full power. A plane maneuvered into position, the cables were attached to the struts, and the anchor was hooked up. Then the plane turned up to full power, and after straining at the leash for several seconds, the catapult trolley was fired forward by an explosive charge. The combined power of the engine and the trolley broke the retaining ring at the tail, and the plane jumped forward, down the deck, to be airborne at the edge.

Usually it all went like clockwork, but on March 1, as we sat on the catapult braced for takeoff, when the engine came to full power a defective retaining ring snapped. We began to waddle forward, too late to fire the trolley, and without anywhere near enough flying speed to get airborne, we toppled over the port side of the ship, down through the catwalk, shearing off metal as we went. Into the water we plunged on our side, under, and then bobbed up, nose down with the heavy engine. The ship high above us went tearing by. All I saw was Cletus Powell leaning out a porthole in the parachute loft where I had just lost seventy-five dollars to him, which I did not have, at blackjack, yelling, "Kernan, you don't have to pay. Get out, get out for God's sake."

No one in the plane was hurt, only disoriented. I made my way out the side of the turret onto the port wing; Mullins came out his door and got up onto the starboard wing. From opposite sides we opened the life raft stowage compartment, located just forward of the turret, and began pulling. Mullins was smaller and less determined than I, and I nearly pulled him through the stowage before he let go. Then he and the pilot came down the port wing. I pulled the inflation toggle and the raft filled up satisfactorily, with a big hiss. We stepped in and paddled off with the aluminum oar provided.

The plane guard, the USS *Massey* (DD-778), which followed the carrier during landings and takeoffs for just such events, had pulled alongside. From the deck of the carrier it had seemed like a light sea, but in the yellow rub-

A crash off the *Suwanee* on March 1, 1945, when the catapult fired prematurely and the plane tumbled off the forward port deck, through the catwalk, narrowly missing the sailors looking on with professional interest at how well we are getting out of the plane. Dyer is coming out of the cockpit with his parachute still on; I am getting out of the turret, while Mullins is crawling up the wing toward the life-raft stowage, just forward of the turret.

ber raft we rose and fell ten or fifteen feet. It all went like a drill until the destroyer loomed above us, letting lines down from the high bow, leaping up and slamming down in the swell. We swept into the side, the raft overturned and drifted away, and each of us grabbed a line to climb up to the deck. As the bow came down and the water rose up, I was lifted up like an elevator by the water, but then as the water dropped and the high bow rose, my weight would come on the line and I would bang down and against the side of the ship. I was dazed and on the verge of drowning, with a lot of water inside me, until I let loose and drifted back amidships where the deck was much lower and more stable. Here I came over the side in an instant and was soon in a bunk with one of the small bottles of medical whiskey saved for such occasions. Next day the destroyer came alongside the carrier, fired a line over, and delivered us back aboard in a bos'n's chair. We were flying again by that afternoon.

Near the equator the ship had begun to heat up, well over one hundred degrees in most of the living quarters, which, on the *Suwanee,* were grim, unpainted, crammed cubicles. Bunks were in racks as high as five or six, the lights were always on, lockers were small, the heads were far away, so that going for a shower—always salt water—or to relieve yourself was a long walk, half-naked, through several eating and living compartments. It sounds like nothing now, but it put great pressure on the men day after day, which increased as the heat went up and we began suffering from heat rashes and raw places where a belt or a trouser leg chafed. It got worse when, on March 4, we anchored in Tulagi harbor, just across the bay from Guadalcanal, and there was no longer movement to drive the fresh air down the vents to cool the lower decks. The heat soared, and the bugs began to make their way from the land to feed on whatever the sea had brought them. We slept in our skivvies—the navy knew of no pajamas—but even so we would wake soaking wet in the morning, glad to get out of a "sack" that was itself damp with accumulated perspiration.

After a day or two we went ashore, taking the planes to Henderson Field on Guadalcanal, where a year and a half earlier the Japanese drive was finally stopped. Now the island was nearly deserted, and we could walk about looking at the muddy jungle swamps and sluggish rivers where so many desperate battles had taken place so short a time ago. There had been a tremendous buildup of American forces on Guadalcanal, but now the fighting had shifted away from the southwest Pacific to the shores of Japan itself. The Philippines had been retaken; Iwo Jima had been recently stormed by the marines; and the air force, with its B-29s, and the navy carriers were at work on the mainland of Japan.

As the war moved on, the troops had simply moved out of Guadalcanal leaving, in that careless, rich American way, their buildings and a lot of their machinery behind them. A library filled several Quonset huts, the books all damp and smelling of mold in the rainy climate, which had only one rule: "If you check a book out, you can't return it." The U.S. Navy

Seabees—construction batallions—had moved out, leaving a big ice-making machine running for as long as the fuel in the tank for the engine driving the compressor held out. Beer was plentiful, huge stacks of cardboard cartons of it, with a single guard walking around. We were in a sailors' paradise for a few days—endless beer cooled to low temperatures in big Lister bags filled with ice.

The pilots had gone off on their own parties, and no one bothered us very much, so we lay naked, except for our white hats, in our bunks in one of the numerous empty Quonset huts on the edge of the airfield and drank beer and more beer and still more beer. Something odd began to happen as we drank more and more. It began with just smashing a few bottles on the plywood floor of the Quonset hut as we emptied them. Then, as the floor began to be covered with broken glass, anyone wanting to go to the head or get another bottle of beer had to walk barefoot through the ever deepening layer of glass. At first it was possible to work your way around the biggest and sharpest shards of brown glass, but as more and more glass accumulated, the trip became more and more difficult and painful. But this problem was countered by rising drunkenness and its attendant indifference to reality, urged on by the need to piss more often and the desire to drink even more beer.

As each sailor rose from his bunk to try to make the door, cheers and groans accompanied him on his trip. If he winced or turned back he was hooted, if he cut himself and jumped in pain he was laughed at, if he strode bravely through the mess into the dark where the beer was—outside the door and the range of the single bulb burning in the center of the hut—he was cheered and awarded imaginary commendations. Young men's initiatory war rites in the longhouse. In time the game wore itself out as people passed out or simply dropped off to sleep. But it started up again the next day, and anyone visiting the Quonset hut where the aircrew of VT-40 was quartered would have thought they had wandered into some madhouse filled with naked men with badly cut feet and blood all over a litter of broken glass.

In time we were all rounded up, with painfully sore feet for a time, and sent back to the ship to the duties we had been transported so many miles to perform. We began by providing submarine patrol for a convoy carrying the 6th Marine Division north for the landings on Okinawa scheduled for April 1. We left Tulagi, without remorse, on March 14, going north to that remarkable fleet anchorage, Ulithi Atoll. On the way north a destroyer pulled alongside with mail and transferred my old friend Loughridge, completely cured of whatever crud had felled him at Livermore, back aboard. Better for him if the crud had kept him in the hospital a bit longer, but no one knows beforehand the turns of Fate.

Ulithi is a huge atoll out in the Pacific Ocean, halfway between the Philippines and Guam. The islands that made up the atoll were narrow coral-and-sand strips, only a few yards wide in places, running in the huge circle around an old sunken volcano, with deep blue water in the center. Here the navy had constructed a fleet base for the final attack on Japan, and as we came into the atoll on our little gray and grimy escort carrier, the by-now almost unbelievable striking force of the Pacific Fleet was stretched out in front of us. Rows of new battleships and heavy and light cruisers, swarms of destroyers, and, in a long row, the new carrier striking force. One old ship was there—the *Enterprise*—and all the old names were there on new ships—*Lexington, Hornet, Yorktown, Wasp*—as well as new ones like *Essex, Randolph, Franklin, Intrepid,* and on and on. It was the most powerful navy ever assembled and a heart-stirring sight to someone who had seen the burned-out battleship row at Pearl Harbor and had watched the *Enterprise*, the last operating carrier in the fleet, disappear over the horizon at Santa Cruz as the *Hornet* began to go down.

Among a forest of repair facilities, an airfield, docks (including a huge floating dry dock capable of taking any capital ship in the fleet), hospitals, storehouses, and so on, the navy's wisdom had decreed a recreation area for the sailors of the Pacific Fleet. Mog Mog, such was its memorable name, was a tiny islet with a small sand hill at one end and a mangrove swamp at the other. As those fortunate enough to get four hours of liberty, myself among them, came ashore from the ship's motor launch onto the dock, a trail led inland to a fork with a sign that said, "OFFICERS LEFT. ENLISTED PERSONNEL RIGHT." The officers filed off up the sand hill to a club where beer, whiskey, and swimming were available in small amounts. Crude but pleasant I heard.

To the right was a gate in a barbed-wire fence where the shore patrol checked your liberty card and nodded at a man standing by a huge pile of cases of beer, who then handed you two cans of the warm brew. Shiny aluminum cans in hand you went up over a little rise and saw the swamp, where by now all the foliage had been stripped and most of the trees and bushes pulled down and stamped into a greasy mash of mud covered with sailors in blue dungarees arguing and drinking their two cans of beer. Here and there a pipe had been driven into the soaked ground and a funnel inserted into the

Liberty and beer at Mog Mog. (*Naval Institute Collection*)

end to make a crude urinal. These were in constant use. Fights broke out now and again between crews of different ships, and there were even a few drunks who had managed to buy their beer from some of the nondrinkers. Mostly, however, even hardened sailors, wild for liberty and drink, blanched at the sight of Mog Mog, and there was—an unheard of thing—a long line of men back at the landings waiting to return to their ships. But having accepted liberty, like mankind getting freedom from God, they could not return it until the appointed hour when their launch arrived to carry them away from this stygian lake.

Within a week we were at sea again, flying antisubmarine patrols for the transports on the way to Okinawa. On March 31 the other carriers of this division, also named after small rural rivers of America—*Sangamon, Santee,* and *Chenango*—joined up with the *Suwanee* to form a division of four carriers designed to provide close support to the soldiers and marines landing on Okinawa. On Easter Sunday, April 1, the invasion began, and we started flying two and three short strikes a day from about fifty miles offshore to the island where we circled until the control on the ground at the front called us in to hit some particular target.

The island was honeycombed with elaborate stone tombs dug into the hills, where the Japanese holed up and kept supplies, and most often our mission was to fly low and come in as close as possible to some particular tomb and then either put a five-hundred-pound bomb or fire one or more of the eight 5-inch rockets we carried under our wings into it. Sounds easy, but from the air it was nearly impossible to make out the exact cave we were supposed to go after. There was a lot of confusion, and sometimes rockets were fired into our own lines. It is hard to convey just how difficult it is to pick out a camouflaged object worked into the landscape while roaring in at 250 miles an hour, staring up a steep valley into a hillside, trying to hold on the target long enough to hit, but with time still to pull up and over the ridge behind. We all worked hard at it and improved with time.

A high cost began to be extracted at once. The air group commander, Lieutenant Commander Sampson, was incredibly keen, pressing his attacks hard to show others the way. He pressed so hard that he was dead in the first week. At the time he seemed to me to be old and grave, but looking back at photos, I see now that he was young, only in his late twenties I would guess, and I am reminded how much the war was the business of very young men.

We stayed only a few days at Okinawa until we went south on April 8 to take over from a British fleet that was responsible for keeping down the airfields on the Sakishima Islands, just off the east coast of northern Taiwan. At this stage of the war the Japanese were flying whatever planes they had in China out to dirt landing fields on two islands in this group—Ishigaki and Miyako—and then loading them with bombs and sending them north as suicide planes, kamikazes, against the invasion fleet and the big carriers off Okinawa. The British job was to keep the fields so full of holes that landings and takeoffs were impossible, but for some reason they withdrew after heavy casualties, and we were assigned to the job, which would go on for months, day after day.

April 13: Roosevelt died. The news was announced over the loudspeaker and brought all activity to a stop. It is hard now to realize the extent to which Roosevelt dominated our world, was the only leader we really remembered. He had presided over the terrible years of the Depression when most of us aboard were growing up, and we remembered him for his "fireside chats" and his reassuring messages about the economy, while things got worse and worse. He had taken us into the war, wanted it really, and we had followed him. I had voted for the first time the year before, and in a cross-grained way had cast my ballot for Thomas Dewey rather than Roosevelt, but now, like everyone else, I felt troubled about who would speak for the country and make the decisions. About Truman we knew nothing, but we had no confidence in him. The days ahead looked depressingly bleak, for we all assumed that there would have to be landings in Japan, and we feared them as nothing else in the war.

The landing signal officer brought a seagull into a landing on board, "Smooth on the controls." But we bumped aboard and were hurled off the catapults, twice a day, early morning and late afternoon, and then once on the next, at midmorning. It became routine. I hated the early flights. Reveille was at four, breakfast was almost always beans, we were launched before five in the dark. There was no time to empty your bowels, and as the altitude increased, the gas of the beans expanded and created terrible cramps. I refused to endure it, a veteran set in my ways at twenty-one, and drove Mullins the radioman up into the turret while I squatted on the floor of the tunnel and relieved myself onto a piece of red rayon torn from a target sleeve. The plane had relief tubes that made it possible to urinate in flight, but there was no way to be rid of my load. Leaving it aboard would have stunk us out, so I tied a knot in the red rag and opening one of the ventila-tors at the rear of the tunnel, flung it out and watched mindlessly out of one of the side ports as this brightly colored "blivvie" made its way down through the second division, flying below and to the rear of the formation I was in. There was some protest about these red rags plummeting down through the formation every other day, but no one cared to push the mat-ter—everyone had enough trouble—and I simply stayed silent.

We made our way down to the islands in the perpetual clouds, dived down on the airfields in the valleys below, dropped our bombs, fired our rockets into the fields, and went zooming out over the island and the sea beyond to make our way back to the ships in the kind of golden-green haze, with rainstorms and bright shafts of sunlight in a dozen places around the horizon, that never changed. It had a magical quality, and there was always a big lift at having survived another run.

We feared the islands, and with good reason. The intelligence officer told us to avoid certain swamps if we were shot down, so filled with leeches that you could die from loss of blood in a short time. We lived in a place and time that seemed far away and vague, a removed and distant place where we bombed them and they shot at us. Where we put holes in their runways and they, with fiendish speed, filled them up again, and we came back and put more holes in the runways.

The antiaircraft fire was intense, and since our job was to bomb the runways we could never attack the guns directly. The Japanese learned in time that we never shot at them, so firing at us became a game, an early form of Nintendo. At the bottom of our runs we were below the ridge lines—the guns were actually firing down at us—and I began from the turret to fire furiously back at them. The casualties continued to mount: April 25, Collura, Powell, to whom I still owed my blackjack losings, and Stewart were hit in a dive and went in and exploded; April 27, Campbell, the commanding officer, Loughridge, my close friend, and Zahn were hit and disintegrated in the air. Death had by then become familiar and almost unremarkable, but still it was difficult to accept that someone you knew well and had played cards with in a normal way only a few hours earlier was now gone forever, not a part of the same world or any world, for that matter, any longer. Despite my matter-of-fact feelings about death, I wrote a sentimental letter to Jimmy's widowed mother in Jamestown, New York. Memory of my attempts to prove that he had lived and died well bring blushes to my face fifty years later. She had the good sense never to reply, or perhaps the officer who censored the mail saw that the letter would only cause more pain and quietly deep-sixed it.

Religion or, more accurately, my desire to be rid of any remnants of belief, was much in my mind those days. I had been a church-going but not a pious young man, and since my mother's death and the awareness that the church cared neither for her nor for me, I had borne a grudge against religion, organized or unorganized. The media and church hokum of the time about there being "no atheists in foxholes" outraged me, since they seemed to say that when it came down to cases, young snots like myself realized what our elders always knew in their wisdom, and in the comforts of home, about the existence and goodness of God. I began to think intently about what was going on and concluded that war's cruelty and randomness, its indifference to human life and the speed with which it erases existence forces anyone who thinks to realize that war is not an aberration, only a speeded-up version of how it always is. The evidence is always there, I reasoned, to anyone who will look and see the plain facts his senses offer him— and what else is there except the historical record, which fully agrees?—that men and women, like everything else in the world, are born, grow and work for a time, and then disintegrate. Where is there an exception? Only the little "I" inside us that, filled with its own vanity, cannot believe it could ever be extinct, though everything in the world declares it to be inevitable. Fear in war forced us to church before battle, and the young man's raw desire to live made us avoid when we could the bleakness of facing total instantaneous extinction. But we all knew it; it was in our faces and it was the basis of our shared attitude toward one another and life.

There was a young Jesuit chaplain aboard who liked to argue about the existence of God, and I took advantage of his philosophy and his youthful good nature to drop in and play the village atheist. Raised as a Catholic, I had always waited for some kind of mystic experience to transfigure me when the host was in my mouth, but I only tasted a thin brittle wafer. The indifferent cruelty with which the Church had treated my mother made me reject it on purely social terms, and now I denounced it in a swaggering metaphysical way to the poor red-faced young priest, who couldn't believe that there were such things as real atheists. He could not imagine that a young man like myself, brought up in the arms of holy mother church, could conceive of a world without a God of familiar attributes. But war had pushed me over a threshold of belief into a hard materialism, and I could never go back. It didn't even matter very much, the shedding of some useless covering that had been kept awkwardly around for sentimental, superstitious reasons.

I gave up tormenting the priest and turned to playing bridge, keeping a game going with the same players for weeks at a time, interrupting our playing on the coolness of the well deck only when someone had to fly, and picking up the game when the player returned. A Boston Irishman named Tom McCue was my partner, a former worker in a shipyard. The waves splashed near us, but we played with all the precise rules and formality of some fashionable bridge club engaged in a tournament.

Although we kept the runways on Miyako and Ishigaki torn up, some planes got through to attack the fleet. We were all thoroughly terrorized by the kamikazes, for it is terribly difficult to avoid someone trying to fly into you. The Japanese always had had a feel for the suicidal charge, and when the *Hornet* sank in 1942, two planes had crashed into her and exploded, one only a few feet from where I was sitting. But by the end of the war the "Divine Winds" had become the only effective Japanese weapon, and day after day the young pilots drank their ritual sake, bound up their heads with a silk scarf, and took their samurai swords into the planes with them to fly out and crash into the Yankee fleet. Being small carriers, and stationed far to the south of the main fleet off Okinawa, we were not attacked for the most part, but every two weeks or so we had to provision with beans and bombs, literally about all we took aboard, at a little island, Kerama-rettō, a supply base near Okinawa. The place had a bad feel, where the entrance to what was the center of an old volcano was a long narrow passage in which there was no room to maneuver. The passage was deep but the sides so narrow that you could nearly reach out and touch the brown rock as the ship slid slowly through. In this situation you were a sitting duck for any kamikaze that came along, and on May 1 one of them took the entire flight deck off our sister ship, the USS *Sangamon*, as she was leaving Kerama-rettō. After that we hated going there even more and went as infrequently as possible, having to fight off attacks each time, but never getting hit.

May 7: Germany surrendered, and the hope of an end to the war got more real. We knew we would win, had known it since Midway, really, but it had all been so much longer than anyone expected that it was impossible to think of it coming to an end. And there was always the fear of the landings on the Japanese homeland. I can barely remember now what it was like always to be somewhat afraid, never to escape that slight sinking feeling in the gut, to awake wet with sweat at night in that unbelievably crowded compartment and hear men here and there crying out with nightmares. Whenever it got better, something would happen, and the fear would come close again.

Sitting at a table in the mess compartment in late May—the twenty-fourth—I heard that sharp flat noise that can only be a bomb. I rushed up the three ladders to the flight deck, and there in the middle, where it had landed, was one of our planes, blackened and smoldering, with three bodies alongside. We frequently carried twelve one-hundred-pound bombs, each in its own bomb rack, to drop in a string across the landing field, to tear it up as much as possible. The racks were tricky, and sometimes in the dive they would not release some of the bombs but would delay until you pulled out of the dive and the bomb bay doors closed and then release the bomb onto the doors. When this happened the arming wire would pull out from the bomb fuse, and its propeller would turn freely until the bomb was armed. We knew about the problem, and radiomen were under strict orders after a run to look through the glass inset between the tunnel and the bomb bay to make sure that all the bombs were out of there! If they were not, the bomb bay was to be instantly opened and all kinds of radical maneuvers were to be undertaken until the bombs were shaken out. But the bomb bay was dark and difficult to see into, and on this day the radioman had missed the armed hundred-pounder lying there because a hydraulic line had been hit by antiaircraft fire and the fluid had obscured the glass window to the bomb bay. When the plane landed, caught the arresting wire, and came to an abrupt stop, the bomb slid forward until it hit the batteries just beneath the pilot, Slingerland, blowing him instantly to kingdom come, and filling the radioman, Joyce, with so many small holes that the serum they poured into him ran right out again until he died that night. The gunner was in a bad way but lived.

Eventually it came to an end. The battle was won at Okinawa, and land-based planes began to take over the bombing of the Japanese southern fields. Planes out of China were decreasing. On June 17 we left for the Philippines and the island of Leyte after eighty-five days at sea, one of the longest cruises of the war and recognized with a Presidental Unit Citation for the *Suwanee*, Distinguished Flying Crosses and Air Medals for the flyers, including me. There was little to do in Leyte except walk around and try to decide whether the cane whiskey the Filipinos sold under names like Freddie Walker, Red and Black, and Three Stooges would blind you as surely as was rumored. We decided it would and returned to the ship only muddy.

TWELVE

Peace

By June 26 we were off to Balikpapan to cover the Australian landings on Borneo. Borneo had been a source of Japanese oil since the first days of the war, and at one time, so pure was the product, they were burning it in naval boilers without refining it. Dangerous, though, and at the Battle of the Philippine Sea one of their carriers, hit by a submarine torpedo, blew up instantly, so volatile was the unrefined Borneo oil. It all seemed wonderfully exciting, passing Celebes and going down through the Makassar Strait, taking us back to those first days of the war when we had felt so frustrated to be unable to help the Australian, Dutch, and American fleet that the Japanese had overwhelmed in Indonesia. Now there were no Japanese to be found anywhere, not even a plane in the air to defend the refineries, and we flew back and forth without dropping our bombs, since the Australians were going ashore without opposition. My last combat mission, if it can be called that, but I did not know it at the time.

July 7, back to Leyte where we anchored and took the planes ashore for several weeks on one of those remarkable coral landing strips the Seabees built all across the Pacific. The strips were a beautiful hard white, made of living coral dredged up from the nearby bay and kept alive by being watered daily with seawater sprayed from a sprinkler truck. So long as it was watered it continued to live, and every day the steamrollers crushed it smooth and hard again. A dazzling light bounced up from that white surface and gave terrible sunburns to the unwary.

One day I flew to Manila, a hundred miles or so to the north, to pick up mail. The way up led across the jungles of Samar where, flying a few hundred feet off the ground, we saw stunning scenes of waterfalls and huge flowers, ten or fifteen feet across, and small villages at the end of long dirt trails. The pilot had business, so I hitched a ride into Manila, which was all mud and ruins. One concrete building alone stood by the river, painted green and offering Red Cross doughnuts, but everywhere else was deep in mud and sour with the smell of broken timber and decayed mortar.

The war was clearly winding down, and for the moment the whole vast army and navy that had come to the western Pacific rested, waiting for the new troops from Europe and gathering strength for the early fall landings on the southernmost Japanese island, Kyūshū. August 3 we headed out from Leyte to Okinawa, arriving on the sixth and anchoring in the middle of the great fleet assembled there. We flew off the field at Naha from time to time, picking up mail, carrying an admiral here or there, but mostly we sat at anchor, played bridge, and listened to rumors: that the war was about to end; that Japan would surrender; that the B-29 Superfortresses based on the Marianas were burning the entire islands flat; that there was some new secret weapon!

By day we would be organized into baseball teams and sent to a small nearby island to play softball against pickup teams from other ships. The worst players were assigned to the weed-covered outfield where some of Okinawa's poisonous snakes lay concealed, which made for the most cautious outfielders in the world. Any fly ball to the outfield was good for a hit, and usually a home run. One day a fielder stumbled over an unexploded 5-inch shell and, shouting for us to look, held it in the air and then dropped it into a nearby well, where it promptly exploded with a loud bang. When the dust cleared, the outfielder was standing there looking dazed, blood pouring out of his nose and ears from the concussion.

Returning from our baseball game another day, we came alongside the ship and began to send sailors up the gangway. At that moment another landing craft came up carrying officers, including the executive officer of the *Suwanee*—a small, dark, mean man—who stood up in the bow, dead drunk, shouting in a loud voice to the officer-of-the-deck, "Get those fucking enlisted men out of there and get us aboard." It was protocol that officers' boats always took precedence in landing, and our boat shoved off immediately, circling while the officers staggered up the gangway after their afternoon of drinking in the officers' club. The gap between enlisted men and officers in the American navy during World War II was medieval, but there was little class consciousness, less so among the men than the officers, who were actually trying to maintain an undemocratic way of thinking and acting. The enlisted men accepted the division as a necessary part of military life, but so American were we that we never dreamed that it could in any way affect our actual status as freeborn citizens who because of a run of bad luck and some unfortunate circumstances, like the Depression, just happened to be down for a brief time. "When we get rich" was still deep in everybody's psyche. But the exec's words, "those fucking enlisted men," spoke of deep and dangerous divisions. He obviously really disliked us, perhaps even feared us, and his words made shockingly clear that he, and maybe the other officers he represented, had no sense of what we felt so strongly: the great dangers and victories that we had just shared, everyone playing his part and doing all that could be done to win the war.

"August 13—they tell us that the war has ended—*Pennsylvania* was torpedoed near us tonight." So reads the entry in my flight log. The word crept around the ship during the late afternoon and evening, half-believed, half-not. We had heard several days before that two bombs of a new type had been dropped on Japan, causing tremendous damage. But we had agreed after much discussion that bombs were only bombs, no matter how much devastation they caused, and that the Japanese were a tough people, about the toughest we had ever seen. It was concluded unlikely that they would surrender, and so the landings were still ahead of us. Surrender rumors persisted, however, and eventually the ship's captain came on the loudspeaker to tell us that there was at least a truce, and that the end of the war was likely. There was nothing to do to celebrate, and I felt nothing, absolutely nothing—no exhilaration, no triumph, not even the simple pleasure of having survived, no anticipation of going home. It was suitable, I only thought, that having opened the war at Pearl Harbor nearly four years earlier, the wheel had come full circle and I was ending it on the last battlefield.

By now it was dark, and around us on ships where the discipline was light they began firing the guns in the air, creating a sky full of lights from tracers and incendiaries. It seemed irritating rather than celebratory, an unseemly, exaggerated response to so long and noble a struggle, an anticlimax in which the end did not live up to expectations or to what had gone before.

We made our way up the Japanese coast, stopping in one small port after another, where, to our surprise, the people were quite friendly and bore us no grudge whatsoever. We felt the same way about them. September 15, the last entry in my flight log records a flight of three-and-a-half hours carrying mail from Okinawa to the ship. I knew it was most likely the last flight and patted the deck fondly when we landed, vowing never to fly again; a vow that I held until the late 1960s, when jets made air travel inevitable. I am still startled by the enormous power of the modern jetliners and never fail to compare the huge, smooth surges of energy they ride on to the clattering engines of our planes that had to be nursed along, every foot of altitude squeezed out on the long way to the target, never enough power to get out of trouble if you made a mistake.

September 17, anchored in Nagasaki, where the second atomic bomb had exploded, a long deep inlet to the town that straggled up the valley and the nearby hill. Aircraft carriers have a lot of space when the planes are gone, and we were there to provide transport for the thousands of Allied prisoners who were working in the mines at the head of the valley. Many of them had been there since the fall of the Dutch empire and the surrender of Singapore. In the end they did not come aboard but went to hospital ships that followed us into the anchorage. I tried to get ashore and got as far as the customhouse. There I picked up some Japanese custom forms and looked out the door for a time at the devastation of the houses and the factories, among which people—in the Asian way of wearing those pitiful surgical masks, like magic protectors from harm—were wandering aimlessly up and down among the rubble, looking for what had once been there. From the deck of the ship we could stand and watch, as we did all day long, the movements of the people going back and forth. The site was not particularly terrible to see. It looked like any other bombed-out town, and there was no way of comprehending that one bomb had done it all in an instant. We knew nothing of the technology involved and cared almost nothing for the morality of using it, the question that has so occupied generations since. The issue may have been raised but only to be disposed of quickly. They had attacked us, we had finished them with whatever means was at hand. That is what war is.

More immediately, each of us felt that those bombs had saved our lives, not lives in general, but our own felt, breathing lives. No one who was not there will ever understand how fatalistically we viewed the invasion of Japan. It had to be done, and would be, but each of us felt that survival was unlikely. Our ship was scheduled to provide close inshore support for the troops landing on the beaches. The Japanese would kamikaze us with every plane small and large that they had left. The fighting ashore would be ferocious, and if shot down, which was likely on frequent close-support missions, we would have little chance of escape.

I had, I felt, lived through a lot, miraculously without a scratch, but my good luck could not continue on into still another year of war. I was now twenty-two, and my youth had been spent in a great war, mostly at sea in combat conditions. I was not, I now suddenly knew, ever going to get a chance to live out my late teens and early twenties in the normal way. I wasn't sentimental about it. After all, my whole generation had spent those years in the service, and it was the great adventure of our time, but I did want what was left of life. *The* bomb gave it to me in my way of reckoning, and while others may feel otherwise, I was grateful and unashamed. In after years, on the faculty of liberal universities where it was an article of faith that dropping the bombs was a crime against mankind and another instance of American racism, I had to bite my tongue to keep silent, for to have said how grateful I was to *the* bomb would have marked me as a fascist, the kind of fascist I had spent nearly five years fighting!

A few days later we worked our way up the eastern coast of Honshū to the great bay of Tokyo, Mount Fuji visible in the background, and anchored at the Japanese naval base at Yokosuka. There was a grim satisfaction in being there, and all around us were the rusty hulls and twisted upper decks of battleships and cruisers that had been sunk at their moorings by naval attacks from the carriers at the end of the war. Ashore, everything as far as the eye could see had been leveled by the fire raids of the B-29 Super-fortresses. Here and there a single cement or steel-framed building still stood, only making the rest of the devastation seem more vast and empty.

Going ashore one gray day in November, I walked around the abandoned machine shops of the naval base. There were small ships, half-finished, on the ways: a submarine here, a subchaser there. Inside the sheds the lathes and mechanical hammers stretched out into the gloom. All, I noted, were built to be worked from a sitting position rather than a standing one. I had, like most Americans, never understood how the Japanese had had the daring to attack a nation so much larger and more powerful than themselves, and here in this grim place, with ruin all around, the folly of their original attack was manifest. It was, of course, pride and blindness that led them on, not any of the complex reasons they devised to legitimate their adventure. It now seemed to me all at once to be clear. Their folly was there, plain to be seen. How could a race that sat down to do their work hope to overcome a people who stood up and moved about while working. Such is the anthropology of twenty-two-year old, uneducated sailors, but at the time it seemed profound.

Despite my young age, by seniority rules my appointment to chief petty officer was long overdue, and I decided, since I would be leaving the service shortly, to push for the appointment before discharge. The personnel officer grumbled about the paperwork, I think he really thought I looked much too young for the senior enlisted rating in the navy, but regulations now required that my case at least be considered, and in due time I was made Aviation Chief Ordnanceman, Acting Appointment, Temporary—about as many qualifications as you can get—which meant that I could hold on to the rating only by signing up for another four years. With flight pay I now earned nearly two hundred dollars a month, which seemed to me like riches, enough that I was tempted for a brief time to sign on again. I bought some gray trousers and gray shirts and a few overseas caps with a chief's insignia; I moved up to the chiefs' quarters: lots of room, real mattresses, special chow, and a mess room in which to sit and read, listen to the radio, or talk.

There wasn't much talk since most of the old chiefs had cleared out already and found transport on some ship going home. Release from service was by an elaborate point system built on the number of years of service, size of family, time overseas, medals, and so on. I had a very high number—more than anyone else in the squadron—but the squadron commander refused to release me on the grounds that I had skills that were still needed. This was foolish, for we didn't even have planes anymore, but he was trying to keep some kind of an organization together, and I was part of his scheme. I complained, bitterly, daily, and was finally told that I could go in late November, but on a group of old battleships that were about to depart on an around-the-world cruise—Hong Kong, Singapore, Bombay, Suez, Gibraltar, and Norfolk. I should have leaped at the chance to be a passenger on such a splendid cruise, but I could only think of getting home, and the three months involved in the trip seemed much too long. So I stayed, waiting in the spookily empty chiefs' quarters for a more direct ship home. A typhoon blew through the bay, and I sat in a chair and slid back and forth across the steel deck as the ship rolled thirty or more degrees. Not another soul was about.

Then the *Suwanee* herself got orders to take passengers aboard (they would sleep on cots on the hangar deck) and to proceed by way of Pearl Harbor to San Diego to release her crew and be decommissioned. It was exciting to be going home for good to begin a different life, and there was a real lift of being, knowing that it was all over. You had survived. You would be a person again, free to move about and make your own choices. But there was cause for reflection too. I had joined the navy in 1941 because I didn't have enough money to go to college, and my intention had been to save enough while in the service to make it possible to go to the University of Wyoming or some college. Now the war was over, nearly five years later, and I had not saved a penny. I had sent my stepfather a couple of thousand dollars by navy allotment from my pay. He eventually returned it all, scrupulously paying interest, when he sold our old ranch, but I had no idea at the time that he would or could ever repay me. Except for the allotment, I had, like the proverbial sailor, gambled, drunk, and partied away all my pay—Jack's a cinch, and every inch a sailor—not that it amounted to much, and now I was going home nearly broke, with no skill—who needed an aerial gunner?—to sell.

But the government had in its wisdom passed the GI Bill so that I was miraculously saved from my own folly and guaranteed tuition money for any college I could get into, plus sixty-five dollars a month to live on. Enough to pay rent, but no more, so that you had to find extra money somewhere.

Among the passengers who came aboard for transport back to the United States from various ships and shore units were some sharks looking for a poker game. We had been running a modest game in the squadron compartment for some time, into which all my recent pay had gone. Now the players made room at the table for the more serious passengers and the game began. I hesitated. Upon appointment, every chief petty officer was given a clothing allowance of three hundred dollars to buy new uniforms. The navy liked people to dress well! I had just drawn my clothing allowance but had only the three hundred dollars to get home and live on until I could find a job. Since I was leaving the navy, no need to buy new uniforms. On the other hand, three hundred was nothing; I would spend it in a couple of months buying beer and hamburgers. Better to risk everything.

You had to show a hundred dollars to get a seat, so I sat down and put my hundred in front of me. The game was desultory and low level for a time, and some of the familiar players from the squadron began to drop out. Then, drawn by the game, the hard-bitten types began to drift in—hairy, strangely clothed, armed with knives, hatchets, and other eccentric weapons. The game began to pick up pace a bit. I won a few hands at first, nothing much, but enough to permit me to keep on playing on other people's money. Once the outsiders came in it became the kind of game where you had always to protect yourself. Any sign of weakness and they would force you to throw down a winning hand by running the betting so high that you would drop out. Money was the weapon, and if you were nervous and defensive, worried about losing what you had, you were done for in a short time. So long as you were playing with winnings, however, as I was, you could, without being reckless, see bets, even outsize ones, when you knew you had a reasonable chance of winning.

Operating in this way, I began to win steadily. Nothing big in the way of hands. Losing often, but winning just a bit more than I lost. Full houses and fours of a kind were not to be seen in the game that night. A pair of sixes would win a big pot over a pair of fours. Sometimes even a king-high hand would win over a jack-high one. The thing was to stay when it felt right and get out early when it was obvious nothing was going to happen.

The evening went on into morning, and the people who wanted to sleep where we were playing, sitting on bunks around a few wooden ammunition boxes with a blanket for cover, were sent off to the bunks elsewhere. But the watchers were as intense as the players for the most part. It was that kind of game. Crackling with tension. There was one other player from the squadron left in the game besides me. A pale red-headed southerner, he whined self-righteously a lot about using the money he had won from us over the last several months to buy a little home for his little family. That money had been stored up in a big roll of pale green U.S. postal money orders, bought at the ship's post office—our only way of stashing money away—and now as he lost steadily, the money orders came out, one by one, a hundred dollars at a time, and were endorsed, each one a railing gone from the porch, a window here, a door there. He wouldn't quit until it was all gone early in the morning, and I suppose I should have felt sorry for him, but all his sanctimony about his family and home built on our money made each extracted money order pure delight.

By daybreak I knew that I had won a good bit of money, but it is considered a sign of weakness to count your money during a game, showing either fear or greed, probably both. So I just kept stuffing the money in my pocket, changing little bills for big ones when the pot needed change, plugging along. Somewhere in the early morning I began to realize that the gods had once again been good to me, and that rather than emerging from the navy broke, I was likely, with a little sense, to come out with enough money to make college a real possibility.

Winners who leave games like this one abruptly are heartily disliked, and there can be trouble in a game this big. Preparation for departure has to be carefully built up, and so about ten in the morning I began to yawn ostentatiously, talk about work that had to be done that day, and then to say that I could only play six more hands, maybe seven, but no more than eight. This was thought fair since, with warning, the losers—and there were some big ones—were given at least a chance to win their money back. It was all ritual, gambler's manners, but it was important, and to make leaving easier I

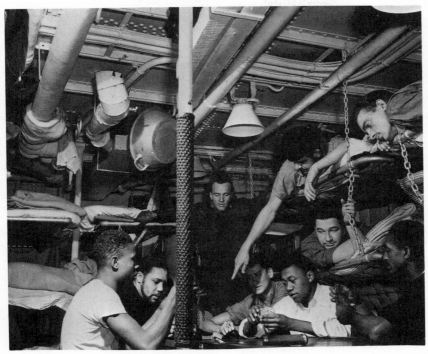

Poker game like that in the compartment on board the *Suwanee*. (*Naval Institute Collection*)

lost some money in the last hands, quite a lot, unnecessarily. I didn't throw in good hands, but I bet weak ones harder than I ought.

Then, about noon, having used up all my chips so that I didn't have to linger cashing in any, I got up and said so long and got the hell out of there. In a deserted corner outside I stopped to count my money. Over three thousand dollars, far more than I had ever had before. Hard to realize now what a fortune it was then. I had played the fool often enough before to know that I had to do something, and so I went up to the post office, paid for thirty, one-hundred dollar—the maximum size—money orders made out to my stepfather, put them in several envelopes addressed to him, and dropped them down the mail slot. I still had several hundred dollars to live on until I got home, and as the ship got under way for Pearl Harbor and San Diego, I got into my new bunk in the chiefs' quarters, where the bunks were always down—in fact, they couldn't be raised—and slept the dreamless sleep of the fortunate. Good luck substitutes for other virtues!

Pearl Harbor was greatly changed. Liquor, not just beer, was for sale in the bars and by the bottle. The lights were on all over town, and liberty went to midnight, although no one cared if you were later than that. The navy was clearly falling apart, everyone was going home, all the rules were suspended, and I only hoped the engineers would stay in the boiler room long enough to get the *Suwanee* back to the States. In one bar out near the Royal Hawaiian Hotel I got to drinking with some sailors from the destroyer *Hughes* that had taken me off the *Hornet* at the Battle of Santa Cruz more than three years before. They all remembered it well, and I insisted on buying drinks for everyone, until we all went our separate ways, for discharge and for home. No one seemed to be staying in the navy.

In early December we rounded Point Loma, and I reflected on what had happened since I had sailed past it for the first time on the way to Pearl Harbor in November 1941. Now the war was over, and I was a different person. I would never again be the seventeen-year-old boy who had come down out of Wyoming in the spring of 1941, but I wasted few glances backward. All the desires pent up by the long years were boiling in me, and I was eager to get out, meet people, go to college, begin, so I thought in my innocence, to understand things. Returning servicemen were gathered in barracks at the head of San Diego Bay and there separated into drafts going to the various discharge points according to where they had enlisted.

Bremerton Navy Yard, opposite Seattle across the always gray and foggy Puget Sound, was where the people who came from Wyoming—not too many—went, and in a few days a draft of about twenty was gathered to go by rail from San Diego to Bremerton. As the senior rating in the group, I was put in charge of it. Not an enviable job. Not all sailors were the kind who had served in the battle fleet, and there were some real fuck-ups in this draft. I was given tickets and cash for meals for the entire group and told to dole out only so much to each sailor at each meal. Fighting with them about how much money they should get at a time was too much of a problem, and I had long had enough of enforcing discipline on people much older and rougher than myself, so I gave each of them their full meal money at one time. The result was predictable. They drank it up at once, and after they sobered up began complaining about being hungry, which impressed me not at all.

In an attempt to get the millions of servicemen back to their homes, every piece of railway rolling stock in the country was hauled out of the yards and

The Old Salt, Chief Petty Officer Kernan, with a four-year hashmark after the war's end. I'm having a farewell drink in a San Diego bar with friends from Torpedo 40, all of us on the way to different separation centers to be discharged from the navy.

put in service. Everyone, even the railwaymen were apparently determined to be done with the war. We were on some old and dusty cars with faded-red velvety seats that had been sitting for years on some siding of the Southern Pacific Railroad and were now made up, as is, into a train. Not bad, though cold, with no diner or any other facilities. You had to jump off at the frequent stops, rush into some diner and take whatever was available, and run back to the train, which would then sit there for another few hours. But no one wanted to risk missing the train.

It wasn't too bad until the second day, when it became obvious that the car was infested with fleas—incredibly hungry, beady, black fleas. I might have endured the itching except that I had taken my shoes off to sleep and been bitten all over the soles of my feet. The itching was unbearable, and as we jerked our way, stop and go, through Sacramento, I spotted down in the dark the neon sign of a drugstore, still open late at night. I didn't want to chance missing the train, but the itch was maddening, so, barefooted, I set off running down the dark street, burst into the drugstore, shouted "something for fleabites," paid for the ointment that was given me, and raced back down the street just in time to catch the last car of the train as it was pulling out.

It took three long nights and days to make our way up through California and Oregon to northern Washington, but we made it at last into Seattle and took the ferry across to Bremerton and the meager facilities of the separation center. A physical examination, clearance of all pay due, a check for the three hundred dollars separation money, a golden lapel button known as a ruptured duck to show that you had been honorably discharged, and then the discharge itself. And so after four years, eight months, and seventeen days I walked out, my own man again, free to determine how I would spend my time and life.

Exactly what to do was not obvious. After buying and changing into a cheap civilian jacket and some ill-fitting pants, I took the bus down from Seattle to Salem, Oregon, where Bernice was still teaching school. She and I had corresponded desultorily over the last year, and I felt that I ought to see her again, perhaps that we ought to get married. This, after all, was what everyone else did. She was pretty and excited, but from the first moment I knew that there were no real feelings there on my side, and after a strained night together I protested that I had to get back to Wyoming, packed my bag, and walked with her down to the bus station. I felt cruel but determined. I had come too far to tie myself up again. She was rightly bitter, and muttering that someone as cold as I was would have no trouble making his way in the world, she turned her back on the bus and walked away. I went home to Wyoming to collect my thirty, one-hundred dollar money orders, buy an old car, drive out to California to see the Boones, and with Dick, now discharged, set off across country to New York, to see what the future held.

In our time there has been much complaint by veterans, particularly Vietnam veterans, that they were unwelcomed and unappreciated when they came home. No parades, no recognition of what they had done by those for whom they had supposedly done it. I think this must be the experience of the veterans of all wars from Caesar's legions to the present day. The end of wars is anticlimactic; no one knows what to do or what to say. They are over, and most everyone—civilians and service people—are glad to forget them. For me, I never wasted a moment worrying about the fact that no one really seemed to know that I had been gone for five years, and the ones who did soon tired of talking about it, very soon. But who cares? What matters is to have survived, to have escaped from all those traps and those people who had such total power over you. To be young and free and on your way seemed a gift beyond compare, and that a grateful government was prepared to send me to college seemed generosity beyond belief. No government I had known or ever heard of had made such a gift before, and I was delighted to accept.

Afterword

One warm spring day in 1946 I drove down to the fashionable little town on the Main Line outside Philadelphia that Commander Phillips had listed as his home address. I got there in mid-afternoon on a Saturday and went to his house, where I rang the bell and then introduced myself to the woman who came to the door, and to the daughter, about my age, who appeared at once. I told Mrs. Phillips who I was and that I had wanted to tell her what a fine man I thought her husband was. She was graciously polite but flustered and disturbed. Neither my clothes nor my manners were what she was familiar with, and she found it all awkward. They were having a party that afternoon and to have some still living part of her dead husband's life walk through the door in that prosperous little town on that warm spring afternoon when things were getting better could not have been welcome. She bravely asked me to stay for the party but was clearly relieved when I said that I had to get back to New York.

I was slightly hurt but more embarrassed that I had not foreseen how out of place I would be and that I would cause more pain than pleasure. Then too, as I reflected, my own motives were suspect. Was I really trying to be kind or just quarterdecking? But the real lesson that came home to me without thinking about it as I drove back up Route 1 was that there was a barrier between the war and life outside the war that was impossible to cross. Even for those like me who had grown up in the war and survived it, the war could not become a part of life afterwards. It remained a vague and troubling presence in the mind, not easily recalled or talked about, certainly not a part of normal experience woven into the continuing flow of life.

During all these years the war has, though obviously not forgotten, seemed very far away. But it was always there in the background, and in the depths of my mind the war has remained the defining experience of my life,

Nearly fifty years later—1993—after a career of teaching at Yale and Princeton.

which I came to think might by now be of interest to my children, and perhaps to others.

My great-grandfather William Lott Peters served through the Civil War in Company D of the Fiftieth Georgia Infantry—the fact is proudly registered in brass on his gravestone—which fought, among other great battles, at Gettysburg. I have often longed for his version of the kind of personal memories I have tried to write, but he left no such record. But using the official history of the Civil War, I once traced the movements of his regiment in that battle. It was on the right wing in Longstreet's Corps, and on the second day of the battle, July 2, 1863, it went down in the afternoon from the woods on Seminary Ridge, across the Emmitsburg Road, down through the Wheatfield, pushed to the north of Devil's Den, and stopped finally at the narrow stream that runs along the base of Little Round Top (known thereafter as Bloody Run), as the battle petered out in the darkness. I have walked along that route and wondered what William Peters, nineteen years old at the time, ever found again in the seventy-three years of his long and prosperous life on an isolated Georgia farm to match the experience of that day. Still, it must have remained locked up inside him, having nothing to do with the quiet productive life he lived, but making everything else feel somehow slightly unreal.

Index

Numbers in italics refer to photographs; references to locations on a map are shown in boldface type.

Continental Divide, 1, 2, 3
Coral Sea, 31, 44, **102;** the *Lexington* in the Battle of, 47, 96, 101
Cowley, Robert, xiv

"Dago." *See* San Diego
Dahlgren, Chief Petty Officer, 10, 12, 14
Dallas, cook on *Enterprise*, 41, 65
Dewey, Thomas, 145
Dilbert, Ensign, 99, 100
Discharge from navy, at war's end, 160–62
Dixon, Chief Aviation Pilot Harold, 39
Doolittle raid, 42–44, 63
Dutscher, 96, 97
Dyer, Ens. Robert J., 135, *139*

Enfield rifles, 12
Enterprise, USS, *36*, 63, 83; accompanied the *Hornet* for Doolittle raid, 42–44; Air Group 6's night fighting off of, 101–22; in attack on the Marshalls, 35–38, 40; in the Battle of Midway, 50, 52–58; in the Battle of Santa Cruz, 68–74, *71;* cruising off Hawaii, 32–34; night-fighting group launched from, xiv; at Pearl Harbor, 22–30, 47, 59; at Ulithi atoll, 142
Espíritu Santo, 83, 84, 109
Essex, USS, 142
Ewa Airfield, 28, 122

F4Fs (Grumman Wildcats), 43, 54, 56, 83
Fighting Squadron Eight (VF-8), 108
Fighting Squadron Six (VF-6), 24, 54–55
Fighting Squadron Two (VF-2), 109
Fiji, **33, 102**
Fijians, characteristics of, 85–86
Flight pay, 62, 156
Flight Training School, 61, 99, 101, 122–30
Ford Island, 22, 26–32, 39, 101
Franklin, USS, 142
Fueling: at night, 27; at Pearl Harbor, 22, 51; at sea, 34–35, 57, 103–4
Gambling, x–xi, 62, 157–58, *159;* betting on war events, 43, 89–90, 98–99; black-jack, 138; bridge, 147; poker, 45, 89–90, 157–59; whist, 82–83

Gardner, Capt. Matt, 116
Gay, Ens. George H., 56
Gearing, Capt. Henry, 19
"Gedunk locker," 83
Gettysburg, Battle of, 166
G.I. Bill, 162
Gilbert Islands, **33,** 101, **102,** 119
Glide bombing, 68
Golden Gate Bridge, 137
Great Depression, the, 94, 153; effect on Frank Kernan, 1; effect on naval recruitment, 16; FDR's leadership during, 144–45
Great Lakes Naval Training Station, 130
Grinder, x, 9, 12. *See also* Boot camp
Guadalcanal, 31, 67; Air Group 8 at, 80–81; deserted, 140; guard dogs sent to, 82–83; Japanese retreat from, 84; marines on, 65–66, 68; Torpedo Squadron Forty on, 133
Guam, 31, 142
Guns: 5-inch, 38, 69, 75, 77; 6-inch, 43; 18.1-inch, 51; .45 automatics, 54, 68, 86, 91–92, 134; 1.1s, 38, 69–70; .30-caliber machine guns, 24, 70, 110; .50-caliber machine guns, 38, 61, 63, 107, 110, *111,* 112–13; 20-millimeter, 69–70, 112. *See also* Enfield rifles

Halsey, Adm. William F. "Bull," 32, 50
Hilo, 99
Hiryu, 56, 58
Honolulu: liberty at, 40–42, 99; Mackay office in, 50
Hornet, USS, 142, 147, 160; in the Battle of Midway, 47, 50, 52–58; in the Battle of Santa Cruz, 63–84; chosen for Doolittle raid, 42–44
Houston, USS, 44
Hynes, Samuel, xi, xiv

Imperial Japanese Navy, 22, 28, 31, 32. *See also Akagi;* Betty; *Hiryu; Junyo; Kaga;* Kamikazes; *Shokaku; Soryu;* Torpedoes; Yamamoto, Adm. Isoroku; *Yamato;* Zero; *Zuikaku*
Incinerator, dangers of, on board the *Enterprise,* 51–52, 58

ABOUT THE AUTHOR

Alvin Kernan is currently Senior Advisor in the Humanities and Director of the Graduate Fellowship Program at the Andrew W. Mellon Foundation, Princeton, New Jersey. His previous academic appointments include Director of Humanities at Yale University and Dean of the Graduate School at Princeton University. Mr. Kernan holds a Ph.D. in English literature from Yale and has been elected to several honor societies. His numerous publications include eight books, among them *The Imaginary Library: An Essay on Literature and Society* (Princeton University Press, 1982) and *The Death of Literature* (Yale University Press, 1990).

THE NAVAL INSTITUTE PRESS is the book-publishing arm of the U.S. Naval Institute, a private, nonprofit, membership society for sea service professionals and others who share an interest in naval and maritime affairs. Established in 1873 at the U.S. Naval Academy in Annapolis, Maryland, where its offices remain today, the Naval Institute has members worldwide.

Members of the Naval Institute support the education programs of the society and receive the influential monthly magazine *Proceedings* and discounts on fine nautical prints and on ship and aircraft photos. They also have access to the transcripts of the Institute's Oral History Program and get discounted admission to any of the Institute-sponsored seminars offered around the country.

The Naval Institute also publishes *Naval History* magazine. This colorful bimonthly is filled with entertaining and thought-provoking articles, first-person reminiscences, and dramatic art and photography. Members receive a discount on *Naval History* subscriptions.

The Naval Institute's book-publishing program, begun in 1898 with basic guides to naval practices, has broadened its scope in recent years to include books of more general interest. Now the Naval Institute Press publishes about 100 titles each year, ranging from how-to books on boating and navigation to battle histories, biographies, ship and aircraft guides, and novels. Institute members receive discounts of 20 to 50 percent on the Press's nearly 600 books in print.

Full-time students are eligible for special half-price membership rates. Life memberships are also available.

For a free catalog describing Naval Institute Press books currently available, and for further information about subscribing to *Naval History* magazine or about joining the U.S. Naval Institute, please write to:

Membership Department
U.S. NAVAL INSTITUTE
291 Wood Road
Annapolis, MD 21402-5035
Telephone: (800) 233-8764
Fax: (410) 269-7940
Web address: www.usni.org